Pipestone

Indian Training Sch.

Pipestone

My Life in an Indian Boarding School

Adam Fortunate Eagle

Afterword by Laurence M. Hauptman

UNIVERSITY OF OKLAHOMA PRESS : NORMAN

Also by Adam Fortunate Eagle
Heart of the Rock: The Indian Invasion of Alcatraz (Norman, 2002)

Library of Congress Cataloging-in-Publication Data

Eagle, Adam Fortunate.

Pipestone : my life in an Indian boarding school / Adam Fortunate Eagle ; afterword by
Laurence M. Hauptman.

p. cm.

Includes bibliographical references.

ISBN 978-0-8061-4114-5 (pbk. : alk. paper)

1. Eagle, Adam Fortunate—Childhood and youth. 2. Pipestone Indian Industrial Training School—History. 3. Indian students—Minnesota—Pipestone—Biography. 4. Indians
of North America—Biography. 5. Off-reservation boarding schools—Minnesota—Pipestone—History—20th century. 6. Indians of North America—Education—Minnesota—
Pipestone. 7. Indians of North America—Cultural assimilation—Minnesota—Pipestone.
8. Pipestone (Minn.)—Biography. I. Title.

E97.6.P65E23 2010

371.829'9707766—dc22

2   3   4   5   6   7   8   9   1 0

*To the Indian children who attended Pipestone Indian Training School
from 1893 to 1952*

Contents

Illustrations

Acknowledgments

I want to thank my former Pipestone schoolmates who shared their stories with me and and brought them into sharper focus today: Joe Crown, Clifford Crooks, Percy Powless, Joe Bebeau, and all the others who rekindled fading memories of the past. "Little Bea" Lammers not only shared her photos and letters but her own remarkable memories of living with her grandparents, Bill and Bea Burns, in the boys' dormitory—along with one hundred and fifty boys! Some elders at Red Lake were eager to tell stories of their early experiences on the reservation or at St. Mary's Mission School, before its boarding school division closed in 1937.

Peter and Jill Furst started me on this trail over twenty years ago and taught me the value of good research and interviews. Susan Hoskins and the staff at the Pipestone County Historical Society Museum were very generous with their time and showed genuine interest in locating documents that covered the ten years I lived at Pipestone. The historians at the Pipestone National Monument and the Minnesota Historical Society made their archives available to me. The Writers Group of Fernley chose the literary style: that of a small boy telling his story, as opposed to an old man writing his memoir. My local editor, "Whip Woman" Gloria Meyers of Reno, Nevada, demonstrated great patience, understanding, and courage in transcribing hundreds of handwritten segments, putting them in some kind of order, and at the same time making necessary corrections.

My special friend, mentor, advisor, and fearless defender, distinguished professor Laurence M. Hauptman, realized the historic value of this book, and makes his case in his wide-ranging Afterword that uses extensive footnotes (a historian's major literary weapon) and forces some authors who may be critical of this work to argue with their own and other published works.

My ultimate thank-you is to the beautiful girl I met in 1948 at Haskell Institute in Lawrence, Kansas. Her name was Cordelia Bobbie Graham. She's a Shoshone from the Fallon Indian Reservation in Nevada, and her father, Bodie Graham, attended Haskell in 1906. In the sixty years of our marriage, Bobbie has been the loving and caring matriarch of the family, sharing cultural traditions and values with our children, our grandchildren, and our great-grandchildren. She's also shown great patience and amazing understanding, and she's tolerated the outlandish exploits of her loving husband.

Introduction

"What are you doing, Adam?" It's my older brother Curtis.

"I'm just writing in my diary."

"You're keeping a diary? What for?"

"Oh, who knows, maybe someday I'll write a book about this school."

Curtis surprises me as he steps toward me and wags his finger in my face.

"Don't you ever write anything bad about this school, you hear?"

Wow! That really gets me to thinking: why would my brother say such a thing to me?

I kept two diaries while I was at the Pipestone Indian Boarding School from March 1935 to June 1945. The first one I lost in the attic of the boys' dormitory. I used to hide it in a space between the wall studs, only the space was open below and one day the diary fell down out of sight. After that I got a second diary, which I lost in Nampa, Idaho, on my return trip from Klamath Falls, Oregon, for my tenth and final year at Pipestone.

Now that I am eighty years old, I enjoy a wonderful perspective of history on so many levels very few get to experience. I've decided to tell about my life at the boarding school as the little boy I once was, as a storyteller in the first person. I chose the middle ground in my narration—not too childish, and not too scholarly. The important thing is to tell the story of life as I lived and experienced it. This book has no narrative flow; instead it is episodic and not all stories fall in a timeline sequence. There are no chapters— just stories. This approach may drive scholars batty and out of their comfort zones, as they expect to read an orderly, disciplined, and structured book. But, after all, this is a book about uncommon events in an uncommon era, which no longer exists. It provides an inside peek into events that occurred and a lifestyle that disappeared over sixty years ago.

Additionally, it is my intent to acquaint the reader with life on the reservation, as well as the mission school during the same time period. Although I never attended the mission school, the older members of my family did. Some of the more horrific stories I chose not to write, because I could not get independent confirmation.

In the 1930s most Indian families had no radios—ours was a crystal set. So our entertainment was visiting, gossiping, and storytelling, because it's with storytelling that the legends—the real history of our people—are passed on from generation to generation. Perhaps I am the only one to take you behind the buckskin curtain to share my life as I lived it at Pipestone Indian Boarding School for a total of ten years. In doing so, I can only speak for myself. Whether at boarding school, mission school, day school on the reservation, or public school, each student has his or her own point of view, whether good or bad. How one experiences boarding school life is a matter of attitude. As I look at pictures of myself as a little boy, I see a cute little puppy dog, eager to please. I believe my positive outlook and attitude helped carry me through some rough times.

The academic standards at the boarding school were the same as the State of Minnesota's; neither public nor boarding schools had any emphasis on Native American history or culture. I had to learn that on my own. It is my opinion that American Indians have been subjected to more social experiments than any other ethnic group in America. The federal government has also passed more laws affecting American Indians than any other ethnic group in America. And no other group has been betrayed so often by a government that we were taught to trust. I cannot go into the complete history of that relationship; I can only give you some of the historic highlights, starting with a beautiful policy expressed in the Northwest Ordinance of 1789: "The utmost good faith shall always be observed towards the Indians: their land and property shall never be taken from them without their consent; and in their property, rights and liberty, they shall never be invaded or disturbed."[1] I thought a nation with a Constitution, a Bill of Rights, and the majority of the people proclaiming allegiance to the Christian Ten Commandments would uphold its commitment to our people.

In an ironic twist of fate, General George Armstrong Custer and his Seventh Cavalry were wiped out at the Battle of the Little Big Horn on June 25–26, 1876, one hundred years after the Declaration of Independence. This was a strong indication that Native Americans would not give up their ancestral freedoms easily. Only three years later, Second Lieutenant Richard Pratt established Carlisle Industrial School in Pennsylvania to educate and train young Indians in order to assimilate them into society. Pipestone Indian Training School was the brainchild of an early Minnesota pioneer by the name of D. C. Whitehead. The school officially opened on February 2, 1893, three short years after the massacre at Wounded Knee, South Dakota, in which an estimated three hundred Indians were slaughtered. Pipestone Indian Boarding School had students from various tribes: Sioux, Chippewa, Sac and Fox, Oneida, Pottawatomie, Omaha, Winnebago, Gros Ventre, Arickaree, and Mandan. Many of them were close to, or experienced, events we now call history. They passed their experiences on to the next generation of students, in keeping with our oral tradition.

Early in the twentieth century the government outlawed many Indian cultural and ceremonial practices. That policy was mandated to the federally funded boarding schools. It included the prohibition against speaking tribal languages. All religious orders were given free access to the reservations to proselytize the Indian people without federal supervision or tribal control. According to S. Lyman Tyler in *A History of Indian Policy*, "On October 21, 1920, . . . Commissioner Burke issued regulations requiring that Indian children at government boarding schools attend Sunday school and church. Furthermore, he told his superintendents to extend impartial privileges to all denominations".[2] Charles H. Burke also reinforced the earlier federal policy listing "as Indian offenses punishable by fines and imprisonment, the Sun Dance and 'so-called religious ceremonies.' "[3]

By 1934, Commissioner of Indian Affairs John Collier's crusade for Indian reform found that many of the federal policies were not working. He ended the Dawes Act, which allegedly was designed to make the Indians more responsive to the land as farmers and ranchers. The Dawes Act's policy went against the Indian belief that no one could own the Earth Mother—people could only use the natural resources she provided. Collier also implemented sweeping changes in the Indian boarding school system and Indian life in general. "No interference with Indian religious life or expression will hereafter be tolerated," he wrote. "The cultural history of Indians is in all respects to be considered equal to that of any non-Indian group. And it is desirable that Indians be bilingual— fluent and literate in the English language, and fluent in their vital, beautiful, and efficient native languages. The Indian arts are to be prized, nourished and honored."[4]

Our arrival at the boarding school in 1935 could not have occurred at a better time; it was just as Collier's new, more liberal policies were being implemented. The Golden Age of the Pipestone Indian Boarding School lasted a brief eighteen years, then the school was closed down in 1952 in preparation for the Termination Policy, HR 108, which was enacted in 1953. The Termination Policy, simply stated, called for the government "to get out of the Indian business" by eliminating all Indian reservations, closing down the Bureau of Indian Affairs, and abrogating all treaties with the tribes. Thus began another sad chapter in the government and Indian relationship.

Now more than seventy-five years have passed since I first entered Pipestone Indian Training School. I have found the few publications about boarding schools to be long on history and statistics and short on life in school, and the personal accounts are limited to the few letters home or brief interviews. This book will serve to fill that gap in a personal way, as never told before. I also feel that the boarding school system has been unfairly criticized for allegedly destroying our languages and culture. Even after Collier's policy changes in the boarding school system that allowed our language and culture, my reservation at Red Lake continued to punish Chippewa children for speaking our language at St. Mary's Mission School and at the elementary school across the lake at Ponemah.

To this day there remain conflicting accounts about life in federally funded Indian boarding schools. Was Collier's push for reform in 1934 carried out as the new federal policy dictated? I really don't know. What I do know, from personal experience, is that Pipestone Indian Training School was carrying out those federal mandates, as the following quote in a letter from Superintendent J. W. Balmer to Gaylord V. Reynolds indicates:

> Perhaps the most outstanding feature of our term at Pipestone was the fact that we tried to make the school a "home" for the Indian boys and girls instead of an institution. Every employee was asked to be a father and mother to the boys and girls. This, I believe, was the biggest factor in making it a very successful one. [5]

We were told that a teacher named Alexander Hart was fired for knocking down a boy.

A poignant example of the strong bond usually established between the employees and the children is this letter written to Mrs. Bea Burns, our housemother, in October 1944:

> Sparta Wisc.
> Ocut [sic] 3, 1944
> Dear Mrs. Bruns [sic].
>
> How are you getting along. I hope fine. I can't tell you how I am getting along. But I sure miss the painting. every time I think of you I start to cry. And tell Jerry I said hi. I wish I was there yet. When I was writeing this letter I was crying to that's all I get to say now. good by.
>
> from
> John Cornelius

Another example of our love and respect for Mrs. Burns is this poem by Roland Nelson:

> *Mrs. Burns is very good*
> *Everyone should like her they really should*
> *She's like a mother I would say*
> *She takes good care of us day by day*

She keeps us clean
And neat when seen
When we're dirty she calls to us
"Go wash up" some boys fuss

That isn't a thing to do to Mrs. Burns
Think of the good habits from here the Indian boy learns

So treat her like you should
And she will know you did the best you could
So I wish you a Christmas very merry
And with your happiness you will carry

I realize there will be critics of my book; however, I will only listen to those individuals who are over seventy years of age and who were boarding school children themselves.

Pipestone

Life at Pipestone Indian Boarding School, March 1935–June 1945

Early this morning my mother runs down the noisy wooden steps, and yells, "Kids! Kids! Your father is sick—real sick!"

I don't know what she means, but my big brothers and sister act like they do, 'cause now they're real quiet.

I'm five years old and this is new and strange to me. My dad is never sick. He goes to work every day. I go upstairs to see my dad. He is laying in bed, and he is white like his sheets and real weak. He says he's going to be okay, and I believe him. I go over to his bed and give him a big hug. I don't understand why Dad's got tears in his eyes.

A little bit later, Uncle Ernest shows up and helps my dad into a car. Then they drive away. The next day I hear, "Tony Nordwall is dead." I know that is my dad. I know my family kills chickens, rabbits, and deer to eat. But this is the first time I've ever heard of a dad dying. My mother, brothers, and sister are crying, because they are so sad. A couple of days later some cars drive slowly into our yard. My big brother Alton and I run after the cars and climb on the luggage rack on the back of one. My mom, aunties and uncles, and friends get out of the cars, and they're all wearing black clothes. They're really sad, and they've got tears running down their faces. My oldest brother Stanley tells us, "They just came back from Dad's funeral."

Things get even more scary a few days later when Mom says six of us kids are going away to a school. This doesn't make any sense, because there are schools right here on the reservation. My older brothers and sister go to one school. And my brother Curtis goes to St. Mary's Catholic Mission School the other way on the road.

"How come we gotta go?" I'm five years old and nobody wants to tell me anything, like how and why did my dad die? Why's Mom sending us away to a school when we've got schools right here? I want to know.

"Addie, you're just too young to know." So are my little sisters, Viola and Gwendolyn. "Your daddy's gone away, and that's all you need to know." I ask a million questions, but nobody answers them. How come everybody knows what is going on but the three of us? I feel like I'm not being told grownup stuff.

† † †

A few days later Mom says, "You boys go down to the creek to fetch water."

I have two one-gallon tin cans with wire handles. When we come back, I hand my buckets to my older brother and he pours the water into the large copper boiler that's on top of the wood-burning stove—the same copper boiler we take baths in. Mom is washing all our clothes for us to take to school. Getting us ready to leave for school turns into a real family event when my aunties show up to help Mom. Sandwiches, apples, and oranges are packed in our cardboard lunch boxes. They say, "Addie, you are going on a long trip, way, way farther away than Bemidji." That means it's really far away.

We're ready to go before the sun comes up. My mom, aunties, and uncles stand crying with my two little sisters, Viola and Gwendolyn. They're saying, "Bye-bye." Viola's holding Snowball, our all-white longhaired cat, in her arms, and she waves the cat's paw to say, "Bye-bye."

Us six kids climb into the big, black, government car to go to school. Miss Kirkland wrestles that car over the deep muddy roads and through the thick woods of the reservation. As we leave the reservation, the tall pine trees look like dark warriors, standing there and watching us go.

I press my nose to the foggy glass window and see the forest change into logged-over cleared lands. Those patches of forests and cleared lands slowly turn into wide, empty prairies that are plowed up for spring planting. It's way after dark when we get to the boarding school hospital. They wake me up, and the six of us are checked into the hospital for the night.

Nordwall children, 1935. *Back row:* Stanley, Curtis, Myra, Alton, and Wallace. *Front row:* Gwendolyn, Viola, and Adam. Author's collection.

The next morning they bring us breakfast and then we're taken to the showers. Oh my! This is my first shower—and with cold and hot running water! It sure feels good. Dr. Williams from Pipestone gives us all examinations. Us boys are okay, but my older sister Myra is kinda scrawny and has dry, flaky skin. Dr. Williams gives her a salve to help her stop itching.

After they give us different clothes we walk over to the administration building. My older brothers and sister go inside and I wait outside.

Ho wah! (Oh my!) I'm in a parking lot between two big buildings, turning round and round, staring at the buildings around me. Some are made of pretty red stone, and some are made of cream-colored yellow brick. It's a huge place—kinda scary. All these big, pretty buildings make me feel real small. None of them are like my log cabin back home or my neighbors' houses that are made of wood covered with tar paper.

My brothers and sister enroll us in school. Then my oldest brother Stanley comes up to me with an Indian couple. "Addie, while we are here at Pipestone, these are your new parents, Mr. and Mrs. Burns."

Oh geez! This is too much for me all at once, and I start to cry. Mrs. Burns takes me in her arms and tries to comfort me. She really is like a mom.

They give us beds in the boys' dormitory. Me, Alton and Curtis go to different rooms on the first floor. Wally and Stanley go upstairs with the older boys. We're divided by age. Mrs. Burns puts me in the first bed in Dormitory Five—the home of the bed wetters everybody calls "Stink Dormitory." When we go down the hall to the dormitory, the smell of stale pee is so bad it turns your nose sideways. Our beds are single-wide, steel frame cots with a thin, horsehair-filled mattress under a rubber sheet. Over that are two cotton sheets, a pillow, and a wool blanket. I am so sad and lonely I can only crawl into my bed and cover my head and cry. I cry so long that I start to remember home. I smile through my tears as I see those happy times.

I remember my last Christmas on the reservation. It was so special to me. I held my breath as pretty Junie Bert tore the paper off the present I bought for her. My reward was the happy smile she gave me when she held up the new pink panties I gave her. My special gift was a twirling top with a handle that I pushed into it. I could pump it hard and make it go fast. The holes in its side hummed as it went round and round. The faster it went, the higher the sound it made. Later, my older brothers and sister put me on a sled, covered me with blankets, and put hot bricks by my feet. Like pulling a dog sled, they pulled me over the narrow snowy path through the woods. We went to our Auntie Anna's house that was full of our cousins. Our uncles were outside skinning out three deer that they killed the night before. Uncle Charlie made that day even more special because he gave me a whole nickel to buy a candy bar. When we got home, we took off our frozen coats, caps, and gloves and stood by our tall oil heater to thaw out. My father put me on top of the warm heater. "Jump, Addie, jump!" The other kids cheered me on, and I jumped into the strong arms of my father.

I cry myself to sleep.

‡ ‡ ‡

I turn six years old on July 18, and the end of summer brings an end to school vacation and the students go back to school, like ducks and geese flying south for the winter. New students and old students fill the dormitory. The sounds of boys crying in their beds prove that I am not the only lonely boy. I could call it the crying season.

All of us boys have to take off our clothes. The old raggedy ones are thrown away. They save the good ones and mark them with the boys' names in black ink.

After we shower we all go down to the basement. We are all as naked as newborn robins. In one of the basement rooms we form two lines that face long tables with sheets on them. As we get to the tables, Mr. and Mrs. Burns run fine combs through our hair. These combs have small teeth that pull out any nits or lice from our hair and we call them bug rakes. When any little bug falls on the white sheet, the boy is sent to the other side of the room where Paul Smith, the assistant boys' advisor, has a makeshift barber chair. He cuts all the boy's hair off with hand clippers.

I'm afraid when it's my turn to go to the table. I hold my breath as that bug rake goes through my hair over and over. It takes only one louse to fall on the sheet, and off I go to Paul Smith. I cry as those hair clippers chomp off my hair. Then he takes some salve out of a wide-mouth can and smears that awful smelling goo all over my head. He puts a homemade stocking cap on my head, but I can tell he isn't done with me. He turns me around and looks for signs of a rash. Sure enough, near my crotch I have a red rash. Another can is full of a yellow, sulfur-smelling salve. He rubs that icky stuff all over my rash. I stink like heck! I dress myself in denim coveralls that're too big and high-top shoes that're too big for my feet.

"Go out and play, Adam."

I go outside and around the side of the boys' dormitory to an inside corner of the building. I put my head against the hard stone and cry my eyes out. Soon other little boys come out, and we're all crying. We're lonely, bald-headed, our clothes don't fit, and we smell awful.

‡ ‡ ‡

Us little guys are too small to play games with the bigger boys, so we make up games for ourselves. We lift a long bench and put one end of it on a big table, making a ramp. We run up the ramp, jump on the table, then jump off the table to the floor, and then go round again. That is so much fun for us little guys. Run, run, run, jump, jump, jump, laughing all the time, until I lose my balance on the ramp and fall on the corner of the table. Mr. Burns hears my screaming and crying and he carries me off to the school hospital. The doctor says I have two broken ribs, and soon my whole chest is wrapped in bandages and tape. Paul Smith gives me fresh coats of head salve and itch salve. With my stocking cap, coveralls, and oversized shoes, I'm now ready for school. I can't even laugh without crying, 'cause my ribs hurt so much.

‡ ‡ ‡

Most of us kids come from reservations where most of our homes don't have electricity or running water. At Pipestone, the first big thing to get used to is how to use the flush toilets. They're terrible noisemakers that can swallow a full load of poop in one giant gulp. Us little boys never flush those toilets at night. I think we're scared of the story of Weendigo, the monster that roars and eats people.

Mrs. Burns in the middle of her boys. Note patches on coveralls. Courtesy Bea Lammers.

We learn a whole new way of life at the boarding school. Lights go out at 9:00 P.M. Wake up call is at 6:30 A.M. We get up, dress, make our beds, and head down the hall to the lavatory to wash up.

Lineup's at 7:00 A.M. in the basement. We form three lines of boys: Companies A, B, and C. Because I'm the smallest, I stand in the front of Company A. My brothers Alton, Curtis, Wallace, and Stanley stand in the rest of the companies by how tall they are. Bill Burns or Paul Smith give the work details to the older boys and then give us younger boys our jobs for the day.

The front basement door is opened and we all go out single-file. I follow right behind Mr. Burns two blocks to the boys' door of the dining hall. The girls are doing the same thing, only they come in the other side. Three hundred of us kids go in for breakfast.

We stand behind our chairs, eight to a table. An older student is at the end of the table to keep us quiet. Us little guys with the stocking caps and baggy coveralls can't look at the girls because we're ashamed. We sure hope they can't smell us. If they do, they'll lose their appetite. We're lucky to be separated by a twenty-foot-wide open space between us.

Our dining hall matron is Mrs. Lucille Blyth, a Sioux Indian from South Dakota. She controls us three hundred kids with a bell—the kind used in boxing matches. Three quick rings on the bell and we all stand frozen at attention. When everybody stops moving, she rings the bell once. We all say grace, and end with "amen." I can't understand a word of our prayer. When Joe Crown comes to school, he tells me he spent three years at St. Mary's Mission School at Red Lake. He says he went to church every day and twice on Sundays, and he said grace before every meal. Then he asks me what the words are that we are saying for grace.

I answer, "I don't know, it's just the way I learned it."

He says it sounds like singsong gibberish, maybe pidgin English, maybe Latin. "I just don't know either."

Joe ends up chanting his version, just like the rest of us.

"Amen" means "let's eat," like *weesinin* in our language.

Then Mrs. Blyth rings the bell again, and we all sit down in a rush. We make a lot of noise. First it's the noise of the chairs scraping on the floors, then it's the clanging and banging of our metal knives, forks, and spoons on our aluminum plates.

Large aluminum pitchers are full of milk for our cereal. Another pitcher has hot coffee with sugar and cream already added. Mostly we get hot oatmeal or Cream of Wheat, and corn flakes and shredded wheat are our cold cereals. We never get any fried eggs. My favorite breakfast is either corned beef hash or chipped beef and gravy on toast. The salty flavor of the chipped beef tastes a lot better than bland oatmeal mush. I can't understand why the older boys call the chipped beef and gravy on toast "shit on a shingle."

At the beginning of the school day, all us kids line up in formation in front of the school building. There we put up the American flag and salute it. We all raise our right hands and recite the Pledge of Allegiance. A photograph shows us with our arms raised up, like the salute of the Nazis that we see in newsreels and pictures.

‡ ‡ ‡

Students saluting the flag. Courtesy Pipestone County Historical Society, Pipestone, Minnesota.

My mom said that the teachers at the boarding school will teach us a lot of things, and I want to learn to make my mom happy. In kindergarten they teach us how to draw with crayons and sing little nursery rhyme songs.

Our teacher reads us fairy tales and stories like "Little Red Riding Hood," and rhymes like "Jack and Jill" and "Little Miss Muffett." That little Miss Muffett confuses us. "Sitting on her tuffet eating her curds and whey" doesn't make sense, just like saying a grace prayer before meals in words I don't understand. I remember the story of Waynebosho walking through the woods tired and hungry. He comes to a garden owned by an old woman who won't share any food with the tired traveler. Because the old woman is selfish, Waynebosho changes her into a woodpecker so she has to work harder to get her food. That story makes sense to me. Nothing they teach us has anything to do with my family. Well, maybe there is one thing, like teaching us how to count. Miss Baker, our teacher, has us hold up our hands and she touches each finger and sings, "One little, two little, three little Indians. Four little, five little, six little Indians. Seven little, eight little, nine little Indians. Ten little Indian boys."

Not long after I get to the school, while I am still real little, I give Mrs. Burns a real scare. She always checks our beds, because boys always run away from school to go home. If somebody isn't in bed the way he's supposed to be, she wants to know about it right away. One night little Adam is gone. The way she told it later, she said, "Adam was gone. I didn't know where he went." And she looked around and through all the dormitories and couldn't find him. She went to the boys' bathroom and he wasn't there either. And she said, "Now where could the little fellow have gone to?" Then she went down into the basement. The basement was almost pitch dark, because only the dim streetlights come in through the small windows near the ceiling. "Barely visible in the middle of the floor was this little boy, just sitting there." I'm just reciting it the way she told it. She said, "There he was sitting with his head hanging down." She stopped in the doorway and looked at him and said, "What a pitiful, pathetic little thing. The kid must be so lonesome." She was feeling sorry for the little boy. Just then, another movement caught her eye. She looked over to the side and there was a big rat, running straight for Adam. She grabbed a broom from the alcove where she was standing, and ran in screaming and hollering and beating the heck out of that rat. Adam just sat there and didn't move. She kept beating the rat with her broom, and then she realized that Adam was giggling.

Us boys had killed a rabbit and skinned it, and after we ate the rabbit out in the parching place, I took the fur and tied it up and added a little tail so that it looked like a big rat. I had my made-up rat on a string, and I just sat there, waiting and waiting, until Mrs. Burns finally showed up looking for me. I made it move toward me, and she saw it. Now it's my turn to get whopped by that broom. Mrs. Burns found out she has a little trickster on her hands.

The next day I tell Mrs. Burns how us little guys hunt rabbits. One way is really simple. We use a four-foot section of barbed wire with a small hook bent on the end of it. Our favorite hunting area is the prairie northwest of the campus. When we jump a jackrabbit, it takes off like an antelope across the prairie on its long legs. Cottontail rabbits just scurry into burrows, into holes under the big rocks, or into woodpiles. Once we corner a rabbit, we stick the barbed wire into the burrow or hole until we feel the soft body of the rabbit. Then we twist and twist the barbed wire until it snags the rabbit's fur. Then we drag the screaming rabbit out of its hole. At first I didn't know rabbits could scream so loud. It's so loud it makes the hair on the back of my neck stand up. As young hunters we get used to it. We stop that screaming as soon as we can by taking the rabbit by its hind legs and banging its head against a rock. Skinning a cottontail rabbit is as easy as peeling a banana. We save the fur to make little toys, like that fake rat I used to fool Mrs. Burns. Cottontail rabbits taste better than jackrabbits.

‡ ‡ ‡

They're always teasing me because I'm the smallest boy and a punch or two can make me cry. Everybody calls me "Crybaby!" or "Baby Nordwall." I hate those names. This is when I really miss my mom and dad and family. My brothers say I am homesick.

As I get ready for my first Thanksgiving, they tell me about the struggling Pilgrims settling the New World. The local Indians brought deer, turkey, corn, squash, beans, and cranberries to a huge feast to honor the settlers.

Here at boarding school's the first time I got to eat fried chicken and mashed potatoes and gravy. We all think it's wonderful. After the meals, Mrs. Blyth sees that us boys don't leave any chicken bones on our plates. We salt the bones, put them in our pockets and all afternoon we chew on the tasty gristle. We break the leg bones with our teeth, and eat the good bone marrow. We never get to eat turkey.

I'm excited about my first Christmas at the boarding school because I remember my last Christmas on the Red Lake Reservation. The school is getting ready and my teacher Miss Baker asks me if I know any songs. I say I do.

The stage has beautiful green and red ribbons tied and hanging all over it. On the right side is a beautiful Christmas tree all covered with lights, tinsel, popcorn balls, and strings of popcorn. A lot of it's made by us kids. In front of the stage are piles of Christmas presents. The auditorium is full of three hundred kids, all our teachers, and all the other school workers. All of us kids are excited. First we have to hear an older kid read "The Night before Christmas." Our school choir sings a couple of Christmas carols and then I climb up on the stage and Mr. Balmer, the superintendent, introduces me as the smallest boy in the school. He tells them I am going to sing a song, and then Mr. Balmer leans over to me and whispers, "Adam, be sure and sing loud enough so the kids in the back row can hear you." I do as I am told and I start to sing.

My voice is kinda screechy, and just like I heard Al Jolson do, I sing real loud:

I went to the animal fair.
The birds and the beasts were there.

My older brothers and sister Myra slide down into their seats like gophers dropping into their holes. I can only see the tops of their heads.

The old raccoon, by the light of the moon,
Was combing his auburn hair.

My teacher, Miss Baker, starts to turn red. But, I'm brave and have to finish what I've been told to do.

The monkey he got drunk,
And slid down the elephant's trunk.
The elephant sneezed,
And fell on his knees,
And that was the end of the monk,
The monk, the monk.

Later, my oldest brother Stanley tells me, "Addie, I'd rather hear you dragging your fingernails across the blackboard than hear you singing."

‡ ‡ ‡

This winter in Stink Dormitory is really tough. They gave us all another wool blanket, but the steam heat to all the dormitories is turned off at 9:00 P.M. to save coal. The temperature can drop to thirty degrees below zero outside. The stone dormitory gets colder and colder as the night hours drag by. Once I pee in my bed, there's no way I can change my sheets or get dry. So I drag my two wool blankets across the aisle to another boy's bed. I throw my blankets over his two blankets, and I crawl in beside him. With the extra blankets we can stay warm even if the other boy pees. The clanging and banging of the hot-water pipes in the morning means the dormitories will soon be warming up. When the hot steam gets inside the radiators, a little valve on one end goes "psst." It feels really good to thaw out after a long, cold, wet night.

‡ ‡ ‡

Most of the games we play during the winter are in the big basement room. The most popular game, because almost all the boys can play at the same time, is called "prisoner's base." We form two teams with our backs to the wall at opposite ends of the room. Boys run and taunt the other team, daring to get as close as they can to the enemy without being tagged and taken prisoner. All the prisoners sit on a prisoner bench on the side wall near the capturing team. The prisoner can be rescued by his own team. We laugh and yell a lot as both teams win and lose prisoners. The game is over when one team takes the whole other team prisoner.

‡ ‡ ‡

The boys' playground is between our dormitory and the gymnasium. We have two great big things made of round steel pipes and poles. They look like two giant daddy longlegs spiders. One has six swings that hang from a long center crossbar. The other big spider has two slides, a couple of monkey bars, and a couple of high swings. Swinging back and forth is boring for the older boys. Somebody brings some wood planks from the carpentry shop and puts them through three of the swings. We make two giant swings, each with six boys pumping away, higher and higher until we can see the ground on the other side of the top bar. We cheer as we see more and more of the ground. Our swing can only go around part of a circle, and when we go too far it comes straight down with a jerk. One time we go so far that when we come down, we are yanked so hard that I slip off of the swing, and try to hang on. We swing down and then up, and then I lose my grip. The boys told me later, "Adam, you did two complete back flips in the air, then landed on the steel ladder on the slides. You slipped though the rungs and fell flat on your face on the ground, knocked out cold!" The boys pick me up and carry me off to the school hospital.

I don't know how long I've been laying here. I hear the high-pitched voice of a little boy hollering at a nurse, "Mrs. Burns wants to know if Adam's dead yet."

How do I know if I'm dead? I remember dead things don't move. So I look at my hand and touch each finger, and I count, "One little, two little, three little Indians. . . "

‡ ‡ ‡

I make it through my first full year at the boarding school, and then we get the good news that all the Nordwall kids are going back to the reservation for summer vacation.

We get home to the reservation, and my mother's got a new husband and a new gas engine–operated washing machine. I like that washing machine best. Mom's new husband is Jack Thompson, a Sioux Indian from Sisseton, South Dakota. He's strong and handsome, but when he gets drunk, he gets real mean. I try to stay away from him.

My mother's pregnant and has to go to the reservation hospital for a check-up. I'm happy I get to go with her. We walk down the hill to the creek with big boards across it that we use like a bridge. Mom walks across, and I stop in the middle to watch some huge trout in the cold, clear water under me. I catch up with my mother. She's in a small gravel pit looking at the ground. She picks up a little grey stone and shows it to me, and pretty soon I find some more just like it. Mom pops one of those small stones into her mouth and starts to chew it. That surprises the heck out of me. Mom tells me, "When white women get pregnant they get a craving for pickles or ice cream. Indian women crave these little stones." I try to eat a stone. It's kinda crunchy and tastes yucky, like dirt. I think that when women get pregnant they crave crazy things.

Right next door to us is Aunt Laide, who has the best home in the area. Mom says they can afford it because Laide's husband, Murphy, is the biggest bootlegger on the reservation. Aunt Laide is very special to us.

During the winter old Equayweg lives in Aunt Laide's basement. Equayweg is a very old and wrinkled Chippewa lady who can't speak any English at all. Sometimes, in the summer, she lives in a little cabin behind Aunt Laide's house and for a long time she's helped with us kids. We've been told she loves all us kids. Aunt Laide has huge geese, and they're terrible monsters. They make nasty hissing sounds and flap their huge wings and stretch out their necks to bite us. We think old Equayweg is the spirit woman for those aw-ful geese. Even though Equayweg gives us fruit and is always nice to us, she's never mean, we still think she is some kind of witch. We've heard about witches, and that's what she looks like to us. She's old, bony, wrinkled, and bent over. She comes up and wants to hug me, and she speaks sweetly to me

Aunt Laide *(left)* and my mom *(right)*, ca. 1936. Author's collection

in Chippewa. I panic and scream and run from her. Sometimes, when she lives in the basement, we can hear her footsteps—thump, thump, thump. The suspense builds up, just like in our ghost stories. The door opens, and the shriveled old Indian lady comes out, smiling with a grin that has many gaps, and starts to speak to us in words we can't understand. When Aunt Laide's there she calms us down and explains to us, and after a while it got to where we're not so afraid of Equayweg anymore.

Aunt Laide has a clock that looks like Felix the Cat. I love that clock. And she has a wood-burning stove with chrome on it that is a wonder to us. In the summertime the women always can a lot of food. There's the strawberry season and the blueberry season—all the berries are used, and all the vegetables. I love blueberries with cream and sugar and hazelnuts. The women get together to put up fruit and meat and all the vegetables for winter. Those times are real family parties. Everybody gets together and shares their food and helps everybody else.

Most of the berries are made into jams and jellies. They are sealed in their jars with a layer of hot wax to keep the air out, and then a metal lid is screwed on. Somebody says they're making wine out of chokecherries, but I'm too young to help. Some vegetables are pickled, like cucumbers and beets. Cabbage is made into sauerkraut. The older people like that sour stuff. An uncle says, "I'll bet you can't think about a sour pickle without drooling." He's right.

Deer and moose meat are hung high on meat poles next to the house. They're kept high to keep them out of reach from the dogs and bears. In the winter the meat freezes, and when we need some, all we have to do is saw off a chunk.

Aunt Laide keeps her preserves and canned food in her basement. We don't have a basement in our cabin, just a little trapdoor in the floor of the kitchen, with a space dug out of the dirt below, where Mom puts her preserves and canned stuff. As far as I know, just about everybody does the same thing.

We have our garden and our chickens. And Aunt Laide has those scary geese. Next to the kitchen in Aunt Laide's house there's a dining room, with a polished hardwood table and chairs. She has a hutch full of china and knick-knacks. We never go into the living room—I remember seeing guns through the door, stacked there in the corner. And I saw a whole bunch of green houseplants.

The Guerneau family lives directly across the dirt road from us in a wood-frame cabin. I go over there and eat turtle eggs with the Guerneaus. They go out to the sandbars on the rivers where the snapping turtles and mud turtles are. And they follow the tracks of the turtles after they come out on the sand-bars to dig a hole to lay their eggs in. Those eggs are like little ping-pong balls. I'm up in their attic with Elmer Guerneau and some other boys, and I try to eat those little eggs that have tough skins. I'm not doing very well. No matter how long we boil the eggs, the yolks never get hard like a chicken egg. They just stay soft and chewy. As we eat the eggs, the boys tell old ghost stories. It's dark in the attic and they scare the heck out of me. Elmer's dad is Jim Guerneau. He paints pictures on deerskins.

We have another uncle and aunt, Sam and Emma Colhoff, that live down at the fork of the road. Emma is going blind with sugar diabetes. Sam and Emma come to visit us and we go and visit them. Both of them are friendly and always laughing. Even in the middle of the depression they still find a lot to laugh about.

The most fun of all in the summer is the Fourth of July Powwow. If my mother can't find me around the house she knows she can find me at the powwow grounds in a clearing in front of the post office. The powwow is done in an old-fashioned way, including stuff like the moccasin game that's a really good old gambling game. It's played all over the powwow grounds. First they put a whole lot of moccasins out on the ground, and the guy who controls the moccasins has a marble, or something like that, and he hides it under one of the moccasins. But, he pretends that it's under some other moccasin, and to fool the other team he looks real hard at different moccasins to make the opponents think that's where he hid the marble. It's up to the guys on the other team to guess which moccasin is hiding the marble. The team goes right through the moccasins until they get the right one, and there are points for how fast they find the marble. They use a little clump of sticks to keep score. The sticks pass back and forth between the teams, depending on which one has the highest score. I remember one time when the game was being played for really high stakes. They could win a horse, or a car, or even a wife! And, there's a singer who sings different gambling songs in English and Chippewa. Those hand drums the players use are much smaller than the huge powwow drums. The beat's a lot faster and more exciting, too. People on the sidelines cheer for their favorite players.

At the powwow I can sit and watch the dancers like Loring Sumner, Bill Dudley, and Dan Needham for hours. All the dancers are dressed in our tribal outfits with beautiful flowery beadwork on them. The bells tied around their ankles sing in time with the beat of the drum. The women wear buckskin dresses that're decorated with flowery beadwork, too. Other women wear jingle dresses. They are cloth dresses decorated with tin cones made from snuff-can covers. Their dance is more lively, because they have to get those tin cones to jingle. They are fun to watch 'cause their butts bounce, too.

I like to listen to the songs. It makes me feel like a real Indian, even if I can't speak Indian. Even when it's time to go home, I'll still be here watching and listening. I can hear the powwow all the way home and at our cabin. I feel strength coming from the powwow. The sound of the drum is like the beat of my heart.

Another thing I enjoy is the powwow smells—the smell of moose burgers, the smell of fried onions. It's a beautiful smell. There is always feasting at the old-style powwows. The women come into the arena with cast-iron kettles and big ladles, and they go around the circle of people and scoop out the food they've made—moose meat stew or venison stew. The people bring their own tin buckets, little lard buckets, or something else so they can get that food and take it back to their camp to share with their families. I enjoy the taste of that meat with the fat. The fatty part's always the best.

Since I'm an Indian boy, I think I'll try to live like the old-timers that lived in wigwams. I can't build a wigwam, but I can build a tent. I use an old wool blanket and build a nice pup tent behind our cabin. When the sun sets the fireflies come out. Chasing and catching them in the field is a lot of fun, and I put my little flies in a glass jar. The flickering of their little lightbulbs makes the darkness of my musty tent kinda homelike. As I lay here thinking about that wonderful powwow, the sounds of those huge drums still echo in my ears.

Suddenly I hear a loud, scary, horrible sound. From my tent I can see across the field to a spooky area with lots of trees and thick brush, which is between our house and the village. That awful sound is like bellowing coming from deep down in a cave. I see lights moving through the trees. The whole thing is strange and creepy. Then I hear men's voices as they walk through the woods holding kerosene lanterns. Then I hear a shout, "A cow fell in the well!"

That pitiful bellowing and mooing goes on until somebody brings a rifle. Bang! Bang! Suddenly everything is quiet. I watch as the lights of the lanterns slowly go off through the woods, just like the fireball stories I've heard.

It's been a long day full of adventure and I fall asleep.

"Addie! Addie!" It's my mother with a flashlight. "You've got to get into the house before you drown!"

I built my tent in a little hollow area, and the water is up to my neck. That warm rainwater feels no different than the pee in Stink Dormitory.

Inside the house Mom wipes me down with a dry towel and puts me in bed next to my brothers. The next morning I pull my cutoff shorts off the clothesline before they're dry.

At breakfast, I'm still confused about last night. I tell Mom, "At school they read us a story where a cow jumps over the moon. Here on the reservation we have a cow who can't even jump over a well. How come?"

My mom can't answer me. I don't understand why grownups have such a tough time answering my questions.

‡ ‡ ‡

The ripe hazelnuts in the bushes out in the woods are a sure sign summer is almost over. Our whole family gathers those nuts and we all carry little buckets or cloth sacks. Those hard-shelled nuts are covered with a green husk that tastes kinda sour when I peel it off with my teeth. Under the husk is a golden brown, round nut. The kids all laugh when one of them says I am as brown as a nut. I guess they're right, because the only clothes I wear are shorts or my swimming suit. I never wear shoes. Back at the house we husk the hazelnuts to put up a nice winter supply.

I take a bag of nuts over to Angeline and Bunce, my aunt and uncle who said "bye" to me last year. They have a nice log cabin near us in the woods. The inside is so neat and clean. It has a small kitchen on the east side, a living room, and upstairs is a high loft that's their bedroom. All their decorations and pictures are Indian. Auntie Angeline especially loves turtles. Turtle pendants made of buckskin and decorated with beads hang all over their walls. Colorful cloth turtle pillows are on the couch. Auntie says, "Those turtles represent fertility and long life." I don't know about that fertility stuff, but I do understand long life. It has to be good medicine. They love the hazelnuts. Then Auntie Angie goes to the closet and brings out a huge rifle—a beautiful .40 caliber Winchester 1886 model. It's a moose killer. She hands it to me, and I look at every part of that wonderful rifle. Auntie looks me straight in the eye and says, "Addie, when you graduate from Pipestone, that rifle will be yours."

Wow! I can't believe my ears, because I know about give-aways at powwows for honors. Now I'm going to get a gift I have to earn. I am the happiest boy in the world. I hop and skip down the dusty path to my house.

My mom's hired a babysitter to watch me and my two little sisters while she goes to Bemidji for groceries. When I walk through the door I see that my older brother Wally is kissing the babysitter. They hear me and stop what they are doing. I stop, and all of a sudden the girl grabs me and gives me a great big kiss.

"*Ish!* (Yuck!) That's awful," I yell as I run out of the house, across the little field, to the woods. I climb a tall pine tree as high as I can go. I sit in the tree the rest of the day. I'm really mad that a girl has the nerve to kiss me.

The end of summer is when we all get ready to go back to Pipestone. This time we have our little sister Viola to share that long ride with us. Mom's starting a new life and new family with Jack Thompson, and everybody thinks it's best for Viola to come with us. Now seven of us eight Nordwall kids are in boarding school. Gwendolyn is still too little to go to school. She can only hold Snowball the cat and cry again when we say goodbye. Now, more than ever, I want to get an education and earn that beautiful Winchester rifle.

‡ ‡ ‡

At school all five of us Nordwall boys pass the awful "bug rake" test. They can't even find a wood tick on me. Still, I'm lonesome and homesick, so I join the little stinky boys wearing stocking caps and oversized clothes and share a good cry.

The late summer and early fall is harvest time and the school has a job for every kid old enough to work. The boys gather all kinds of vegetables—potatoes, turnips, carrots, and beets—that we store in two big root cellars. The girls can everything else that they keep in the huge kitchen basement. My older brother Stanley took a photograph of Viola dressed in a chef's hat and wearing a white apron. She looks proud and is holding a big jar of pickled cucumbers. Her beautiful smile tells us she's getting over her homesickness.

Oh boy, we have a new baker! I don't know if Mrs. Trottachaud retired or died from eating her own bread. Her bread was flat and heavy, and made a loud clunk when I dropped a piece of it on my plate. She didn't like to use yeast to make it rise. She said yeast was too expensive. Harlan Bushyhead, a Southern Cheyenne, just graduated from Haskell Institute, and he's our new baker. He says, "By God, you kids deserve good bread, and I'm going to give you good bread." After that, everything he makes in that bakery tastes a whole lot better.[1]

The squealing pigs at the pig farm is a sure sign it's time to butcher the hogs. We have over two hundred. Mr. Brush selects a couple to be butchered and processed in time for the fall semester at school. As I watch the bloody process, I can tell it's a little different from how my uncles dress out a deer on the reservation. Here every part of a pig is used. The head is made into headcheese or souse. The guts are cleaned out to use to make sausage. Hams and bacon are smoked and cured. Even the feet are used to make pickled pigs feet. The rest of the meat is cut into roasts, pork chops, or rib chops. I really love eating boiled pig tongue or heart. The old-time Indians say that eating a heart will make you brave and strong.

We have forty-two milk cows and two huge breeding bulls: Ferdinand and Zippy. Mr. Brush has noticed Ferdinand, who's really old, is more interested in smelling the flowers than the hind end of cows. Mr. Brush buys a younger, stronger bull named Pat to take Ferdinand's place. That big old bull doesn't have a clue about what is going to happen to him. Mr. Brush leads Ferdinand to a big tree behind the barn. Mr. Brush hits Ferdinand in the middle of his forehead with a sixteen-pound sledgehammer. All four of his legs stiffen and spread out. His huge body hits the ground with a loud thump. Then we hang him in that tree with a block-and-tackle. As they gut him out everything that we can eat is set aside. I can smell the hot blood and guts. After they skin and quarter him, they hang those huge chunks of meat in the walk-in cooler to cure.

When somebody said "tough meat," they must've meant Ferdinand. No matter how long they steam cook that meat it just won't get tender. That bull meat is muscle clear to the bone. Three hundred Indian boys and girls have to gnaw and tear at that tough meat like a pack of wolves. I grab the huge leg bones, scoop out the marrow, and then spread it on soft bread and add a little salt and pepper. It's delicious. The boys lucky enough to get a two-inch-long piece of muscle, sprinkle salt on it and put it in their pockets. All afternoon they'll tear off little pieces with their teeth and chew and chew. We call it Indian gum.

Ferdinand's replacement, Pat, is up to his job. One night he broke out of his pen and had his choice of forty-two cows, all standing in their stalls, held in by stanchions. At the morning milking time, Mr. Brush herded the tired bull back to his pen. He says next spring we'll have a bumper crop of calves.

When Ferdinand couldn't do his job, we ate him. When the cows stop giving milk, we eat them. When we have too many baby bulls in the spring calves, we eat them.

With the pigs it doesn't matter what kind they are, when they get big enough, we eat them. The pork we get at school always seems to have a lot of gristle. Lots of times we get skin with lots of hairs on it still on the meat. Everybody has to pick out the hairs as we eat. The hide is the toughest part, and most of us boys salt it and save it so we can chew on it all afternoon.

At the boarding school the only animals we don't eat are the horses. They're huge Belgian workhorses that pull the plows, wagons, and drag buckets. I think they've got as much meat on them as Ferdinand. The Sioux boys tell me that when the most of the buffalo were killed on the plains, the government gave horses to the Indians to eat. I feel cheated because I can't be like the Sioux and eat horse.

The late summer's always busy. We get our class assignments and our work details. We're all given responsibility because it takes a group effort to help out the school. No matter what the job is, us boys can always find a way to make a game of it.

My older brother Wally and his crew have to rake the leaves in the parking lot. Wally hunkers down as small as he can and the other boys cover him with leaves. He looks like all the other piles. Just then Superintendent Balmer comes from town and drives over a big pile of leaves and parks in his usual spot. He can't understand what all the hollering is about. Wally screams under the car, and Mr. Balmer finds out he has parked his car on top of a boy. The boys run to find the car jacks, and they lift the car off my crying brother. The car axle is like a huge bear paw that clawed across my brother's back. He is bleeding badly. We carry Wally off to the school hospital, and the doctor stitches him up. They keep him in the hospital for two weeks, and I don't think he's ever going to heal. I guess the good thing is that Wally doesn't have to rake any more leaves this fall.[2]

‡ ‡ ‡

Me *(center)* making mats for Christmas presents in Miss Riddle's fifth-grade class. Courtesy Pipestone County Historical Society, Pipestone, Minnesota.

It seems as though everybody at school is getting ready for the big Christmas pageant they call "The Nativity."[3] A lot of that stuff I don't understand, but it sure sounds good. Almost everybody in the school is taking part in the big event. My older brother Curtis is playing Gabriel, and my brother Alton is one of the shepherds. Our boys' advisor is one of the wise men, and our school principal Art Bensell and Pemberton Doxtator are the other two. They all look kinda goofy with their fake beards and long robes. I'm wearing a robe, too, and I'm singing in the choir, only now I know not to sing so loud and screechy. My sister Myra has it good. All she has to do is sit in the audience and enjoy the long, long program. But, it's worth the wait.

After the show and all the applause, Mr. Bensell shouts, "Everybody be quiet! I think I hear Santa Claus coming."

Sure enough, we can hear sleigh bells outside the auditorium. All our giggling and laughs change into cheers when Santa Claus walks through the side door next to the stage. He's carrying a huge bundle on his back and he's shouting, "Ho! Ho! Ho!"

We all sing "Santa Claus Is Coming to Town," and I've never heard so many happy voices sing that song together before. I look at the fat man all dressed in red trimmed with white fur. He's wearing black boots and a pointy red cap with a big white tassel on it. You know, that Santa Claus looks a lot like our superintendent, J. W. Balmer. Santa Claus calls to his elves to read out the names on the Christmas packages.

Every student gets at least one package; the lucky ones get two or three. Mr. Bensell tells us, "Don't open the presents here. Wait until you get to your dormitories."

As we file out of the auditorium, the girls on the right side and the boys on the left side, we are each given a green or red mesh sack full of candy, nuts, an orange, and an apple. We don't notice the freezing air as we run back to the boys' dormitory. We all go to the basement to open our gifts. The boys all whoop and holler as they tear open their presents.

My mother sent a box of candy for Curtis, Alton, and me to share. It's full of fudge and white divinity candy. Boy! Our mom can make the best divinity candy in the whole wide world. This has been the biggest and best Christmas I've had. Boy, I can hardly wait until next Christmas.

‡ ‡ ‡

When school lets out for the year and we get a chance to go back to Red Lake, we don't know what's going to happen. Our mom's moved to Sisseton, South Dakota, to be with her Sioux husband, Jack Thompson. She's left our family and friends to take care of us kids. My brother Alton and I get to go stay with Grandpa and Grandma Lussier at their little farm next to the Clearwater River on the west side of the reservation. They have all kinds of stuff like a canoe and fishing spears with shafts that are over ten feet long. Their barn is the strangest barn I've ever seen. It's dug out of the big riverbank. The roof's made of logs covered with a lot of dirt. Grandpa says it keeps the cows and horses cool in the summertime and warm in the winter. It looks like a great big cave to me.

Grandpa Adam and Grandma Mary have twelve children. The oldest ones are married and moved away. I'm two years older than my youngest aunt, Aunty Patsy.

Just like at Pipestone, at Grandpa and Grandma's everybody has chores to do. We have to milk the cows, slop the hogs, feed the chickens, and work in the gardens. Uncle Dicky pours the milk into a big bowl on top of the separator, and I turn the crank. Soon cream's coming out of one spout and skim milk comes out of the other. Grandma's taught Alton and me how to churn butter. We have to do everything by hand, because there's no electricity or running water like there is at the boarding school. Grandma and Grandpa don't have a refrigerator or icebox, so we carry the milk, cream, and butter, and any other things we need to keep cold out to the well. There's one rope for the water bucket, and other ropes have boxes hanging on them. We fill the boxes and lower them into the deep cold well. We stop just above the water.

When we finish our chores all us kids get to go swimming in the river. We have a rope tied to a high tree branch and we can swing way out and drop in the water with a big splash. Boy! That looks fun! It's fun, too, digging for clams in the sand in the bottom of the shallow river. Everybody tries to dig the most. The girls always beat Alton and me. Heck, they've done it a lot before, but this's the first time for Alton and me. Grandma sure is happy with the big cans we bring her full of clams, and she's cooked them for a big clam feed. The older ones eat the clams, but the idea of eating a slimy clam doesn't sound good to us kids. So us kids get a special treat—a thick coat of lard spread on homemade bread with a little bit of salt sprinkled on top. Besides, we always have plenty of deer and moose meat to eat.

All us kids sleep in the upstairs loft in the farmhouse. The mattresses, pillows, and quilts are all stuffed with goose and duck down. They're soft and warm, nothing like the hard horsehair mattresses at boarding school. All the men in the family are good hunters and every fall duck season they save all the down for stuffing.

Once a week my aunties change the bedsheets and pull back the mattresses so we all can pick the bedbugs out of the seams. They spray kerosene on the bunches of bedbugs that hide in the inside corners of the bed frame. You know those bedbugs don't only bite, they stink, too!

One day at sunset Grandpa says, "All right kids, everybody in the car!"

My aunties and uncles are all excited and happy because they all know what's going to happen.

I don't know how Grandpa can see to find his way through the dark woods on that small dirt road. I guess it doesn't matter, because everybody in the car is singing.

Be sure it's true when you say I love you.
It's a sin to tell a lie.
Many a heart has been broken.
Just because those words were spoken.
I love you, yes I do, believe me.

Grandpa slams on the brakes just in time to miss a huge bear that's crossing the road. Grandpa says, "My God! That bear must weigh at least five hundred pounds!"

When we get to Grandpa's hunting cabin next to a small lake, there's a big bonfire and other people in my family are already there. They put Coleman lanterns outside and kerosene lamps inside of the cabin. Grandpa and Uncle Charlie had made a big batch of home-brew beer before, and now it's time for a party.

The men of our family always have big hunting dogs, like black Labradors and golden retrievers. It's fun throwing sticks out into the lake for the dogs to swim after and bring back. When we pet the dogs we find big grey wood ticks the size of grapes sticking to their skins. We twist and pull the ticks off the dogs and throw them into the bonfire. They pop from the heat. *Ish!*

Summer's almost over, so it's time for Grandpa and Grandma to make a big shopping trip to Bemidji to pick up supplies for the winter. All us kids are loaded into a car called a Whippet, and away we go on another adventure—shopping in big stores.

On the trip back to Clearwater, the car is so full I am sitting on the floorboard squeezed between my grandma's feet. Down here I can talk to Grandpa and watch him wrestle with the steering wheel. He calls me "Weh-eh." That's a name I've never heard before. My name's Adam Nordwall and the boys at the boarding school call me Snortwall, Nordy, Baby Nordwall, and other names that hurt my feelings. Now Grandpa calls me Weh-eh.

"Grandpa, why do you call me Weh-eh?"

"'Cause that's what you are, my *weh-eh,* my namesake. You carry my Indian name Amabese, it was my father's name. It was my grandfather's name. And, now it's been passed on to you."

I'm really excited, and I say, "Oh wow! I've got an Indian name, Amabese. What does it mean Grandpa?"

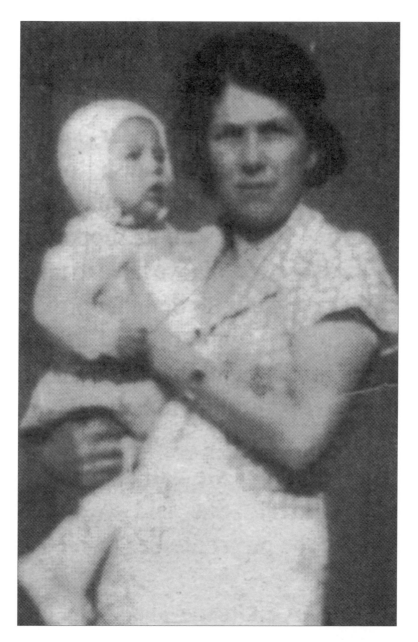

Mom and her ninth child, George Thompson, ca. 1937. Author's collection.

"It means *handsome*. It's your boyhood name." Grandfather then says something in Chippewa that I don't understand. The only word I understand is *migizi*, that means eagle. "That is your manhood name and you can't use it until you become a man," answered Grandfather.

Oh, geez! I must be blushing because my ears are getting hot. Grandpa, Grandma, and all my aunties are laughing at my embarrassment. I can't tell any of the other boys at school that I have an Indian name that means "handsome." The other boys will tease the heck out of me if they find out my name is Handsome. But that's okay as long as I know that I have Indian names and my grandfather knows my names and that's a secret between just the two of us.

I hear a huge bang! Somebody yells, "Blow out!"

Grandpa hears that and he pulls over to the side of the road.

"Dagnab it!" is about the worst cuss word he says in front of us kids. While Grandpa, Uncle Charlie, and Uncle Jimmy bring out the tools, the women get out the picnic baskets. The men soon have the Whippet jacked up and the tire and rim pulled off, and they find the hole in the inner tube. Every car on the reservation has a tire patch kit. Grandpa takes some sandpaper and roughs up the area around the hole, then he smears some sticky stuff around it. The tire patch has a metal backing filled with something like gunpowder. When Grandpa lights it with a match, it heats up the rubber patch and makes it stick to the inner tube. I think they call it vulcanizing. That inner tube has ten other patches on it. The men stuff the inner tube back into the tire, then they mount it on the wheel. They take turns pumping up the tire, and soon we pack up everything and get back on the road.

‡ ‡ ‡

I'm in second grade now, and next to my desk on the wall is a pretty little girl who is smiling. She has on a white apron, wood shoes, and a little white cap that looks like a bird with open wings. She's standing in beautiful tulips and behind her are windmills. Across the bottom of the poster are large letters that spell HOLLAND. I have no idea what Holland is, but if it has all pretty girls like that, it must be a nice place to be.

Now, I really like to draw and paint. My teacher, Miss Tedrow, is really proud of a giraffe I drew, and she pasted it in the window of our classroom door. Then I drew two Indians in a canoe getting wild rice. She put that one on our bulletin board. I really like everybody saying they like my pictures.

There's a new boy at school and everybody calls him Dopey. He looks like Dopey in that *Snow White and the Seven Dwarfs* movie. His ears are big and floppy and he has a big wide grin. He looks just like Snow White's Dopey.

Us boys explore and know everything around the boarding school. North are huge granite boulders sticking out of the ground. Some of them have their sides polished by the buffalos rubbing and scratching themselves on them. We can still see buffalo wallows where they rolled and rolled in the dirt in a great big dust bath. I find a big round stone with grooves in it. I show it to Mr. Brush, our school farmer. He tells me that it was a big stone hammer used to kill the wounded buffalo. I give him that stone war club.

⁙ ⁙ ⁙

Every Sunday we all have to go to church. Church is something I don't understand. My Aunt Anna told me my father was Evangelical, my brother Curtis is Catholic, and my mother and other three older brothers and sister are Episcopalian. On Sunday morning Mrs. Burns asks me what faith I belong to. I say, "Chippewa."

She just laughs. "Well, young man, you're going to church."

"Oh geez, do I have to?"

"You don't have a choice."

In the basement is the storeroom where over two hundred suits are on hangers. Mrs. Burns picks out one that's my size, and I dress up in my Sunday best.

The Catholics go to church in the school auditorium. The rest of us are put on a bus to town and we're dropped off at different churches. We have to know when to sit down, when to stand up, when to kneel down, when to sing, when to pray and when to keep quiet to hear Reverend Johnson preach on and on and on. We say "amen" a lot, just like at our meals at the school. I still don't know the words to grace, only "Amen, let's eat!" The big difference is when we say "amen" at church they don't feed us.

I ask Reverend Johnson, "How come there's more Catholics at school than Episcopalians?"

He tells me, "Catholic priests and missionaries came out west with the explorers and the military. They rode on horses or in wagons. The Episcopalians waited until the railroads were built. That's why we have less Episcopalians."

That makes sense to me.

‡ ‡ ‡

It always seems that us little guys like to play in dirt and get messy, and Mr. and Mrs. Burns are always trying to keep us clean. Every morning before breakfast we all have to wash up and comb our hair. The older boys use pomade to slick down their hair like Rudolph Valentino or George Raft in the movies. After breakfast we take our toothbrushes from a big rack and use tooth powder to brush our teeth. When we run out of tooth powder, we use salt. Now we're ready for school.

Every Saturday we take showers and wash our hair. Mrs. Burns doesn't trust us little guys. We just get wet and pretend we're clean. Before we put on our clothes, she checks us over. If she sees any dirt at all we're sent back to the showers. She looks behind our ears, at our elbows and knees, and, oh geez, she makes us bend over. I tell her, "Only my mom can look at my bare butt."

She says, "I'm the boss now, be quiet and bend over!"

Mrs. Burns is not only looking for dirt, she's looking for that awful red rash we call "the itch." She has a big can of salve with her on shower days. Her sharp eyes can spot a rash clear across the shower room. She globs that gooey stinky stuff all over the rash. After two or three times the rash will go away. Boy, it feels so good when the rash goes away and we don't itch and scratch anymore. And better yet, we don't stink so bad.

After we shower she gives us clean clothes.

When I first got here the soap we used was yellow-brown lye soap that was so strong that it burned our skin when we washed with it. None of us boys liked to wash up or to take a shower. Everything's changed now that we have big white bars of Ivory soap. They make lots of suds, and they float!

Behind the showers is a trough that goes to a drain. Bars of Ivory soap float down to the drain, and we pick them up and run back into the shower. We wash a little and let the soap squirt out, and the trip starts all over again.

We can carve that Ivory soap into little buffalos, bears, pistols, and boats. When we carve a boat we stick a sucker stick in it and put on a paper sail. It's a lot of fun watching those boats bobbing down our river drain. Now taking a shower is fun and we play long enough in the shower to soak all that dirt off. We go back to the dormitory with clean hands and faces. Mrs. Burns is so proud of us, but one day Dopey Sayers hollers out, "Hey, Mrs. Burns, you can look at my butt now. It's nice and clean."

Darn that Dopey! He must enjoy being whipped with that leather strap. Once we get to the third grade, she'll stop checking our butts.

‡ ‡ ‡

Thanksgiving, Christmas, and New Year's Day are the best meals of the year and they're the most fun. We get fried chicken, mashed potatoes, gravy, green beans, celery, salad, hot rolls, pumpkin pie, milk and coffee. What makes it even more special is that the teachers and the workers serve us kids on Thanksgiving and Christmas. On New Year's Day it's our turn to serve them. We're like a great big family. We never get turkey at Thanksgiving. Most of us don't know what a Thanksgiving turkey is. We only read that Indians fed that bird to the Pilgrims over two hundred and fifty years ago. Instead, we get fried chicken.

Mr. Balmer, our superintendent, is on a business trip in northern Minnesota and decides to do something special for us kids on Thanksgiving. He brings back fifty pounds of Mahnomen wild rice because he knows that it's a traditional food of us Chippewas.

Mr. Balmer smiles when he serves the tray of food to us. When he sees one of the Chippewa boys shoving the plate of rice off to the side of the tray, he asks the boy, "Why're you doing that?"

The boy answers, "That's all I get at home. I'm sick of it!"

Poor Mr. Balmer.

‡ ‡ ‡

My older sister Myra stops me in the hallway before class starts. "Viola's sick in bed, and Miss Freeman won't take her to the hospital. She says Viola's only pretending to be sick to get out of class."

Viola loves school and learning new things, so this doesn't make any sense to me. The next day they tell me that Viola's in the school hospital. They say she's really, really sick. The school sends a telegram to my mother at Sisseton telling her to come to the school right away. It's Easter and I go to visit Viola in the hospital. I'm taking her a little basket with little colored candy eggs in a nest of shredded paper that looks like grass. I give that basket of candy eggs to Viola and watch my little sister slowly eat each egg. She's so happy it makes my body tingle.

That night my mother and older members of the family sit on benches in the hospital hallway. Viola dies that night from "sleeping sickness."[4] My oldest brother, Stanley, tells me, "You could hear her heartbeat down the hallway as she tried to stay alive." I feel guilty that I made her die by giving her my candy Easter eggs.

The next day Mom and us kids have to go to town to pick out a casket for Viola. While we're there I smell a different kind of flower I've never smelled before. Now, every time I smell those flowers, I think of my little sister Viola and feel guilty. I feel like I killed her, because I gave her those little candy Easter eggs just a few hours before she died. I cry my eyes out, but that doesn't bring back my little sister.

‡ ‡ ‡

In the basement of the boys' dormitory is a small room that the older boys say is where they keep the runaway boys locked up. Maybe it's to scare us, because I haven't ever seen that room used like that. Really, the room's got our good suits on hangers on racks along two walls. The other end of the room we call the candy room. Every Saturday morning any boy with a nickel or dime can buy a pop or candy bar there. Paul Smith, the assistant boys' advisor runs the candy store, and one day he says, "Hey, you boys, I'll give a free candy bar to the one who can hang on the pipes the longest!"

Like a bunch of monkeys, we jump up and grab ahold of the pipes that hang from the ceiling. Paul Smith gets a good laugh as the boys lose their grips on the pipes and fall down on the floor one by one. Most of the boys hold their hands side by side, but I overlap my hands and lock my knuckles together. I can hang there until my arms go dead, because I sure want to win that candy bar. If I have to, I can hang on all day. Dopey Sayers lets out a yell and drops off the pipe. That makes me the winner.

Ho wah! (My goodness!) I look at all those different candy bars on the counter, all in their own boxes: Snickers, Milky Way, Mounds, Three Musketeers, Bit-O-Honey. I pick a Hershey's chocolate bar with almonds. I want to enjoy this chocolate bar as long as I can, so I take small bites and let that chocolate slowly melt in my mouth. When I get to an almond is the only time I chew. Other boys can eat a whole candy bar while I melt and enjoy a tiny bite.

We like to play and have fun, and so we need toys. We can't buy fancy wind-up toys from J. C. Penney's or Woolworth's five-and-ten-cent store in town, so we make our own. We take an empty thread spool, button, rubber band, and a sucker stick and make our own windup toys. We carve pieces of sugar pine into airplanes with propellers that spin when the wind hits them. We glue a string to the wingtip and our airplane flies round and round as we hold onto that string. We get kind of fancy when we fly two planes at once.

‡ ‡ ‡

A white couple is camped out at the quarry at Pipestone National Monument, and they see some of us boys catching and playing with big crawdads in the creek. They're four or five inches long.

The man yells, "Hey, you boys. I'll give you a penny apiece for each one you catch for us."

Oh, wow! Five crawdads will buy one candy bar!

We turn over every flat rock in the creek and catch a couple dozen of those mudbugs. We carry our catch back to their camp in one-gallon tin cans and we see the couple have a fire going and a stew pot full of water heating on it. She's peeling and slicing potatoes and throwing them in the pot. The man pays us our twenty-five cents for the crawdads, and we wait around to see what they're going to do with them. We crawl up on the rocks and watch them.

We can't believe it when he dumps the live crawdads into the pot of boiling water. I imagine those crawdads burning and kicking and screaming when they hit that boiling water. There's no way we're going to leave now. We have to know what's going to happen next. When the crawdads turn red the man says to the woman, "They're ready now."

We watch them take a crawdad and break it in half with their fingers. They suck the juices out of the head part and split the tail part open to eat the meat inside.

"*Ish! Ish!*" (Yuck! Yuck!), says one Chippewa boy. We watch the white couple eat all the crawdads. When we get back in time for supper in the dining hall, it doesn't seem so bad. We're getting boiled pig meat with skin and hair still on it. At least we kill it before we cook it.

‡ ‡ ‡

We're getting ready for summer vacation, and Mr. Burns tells us Nordwall kids, "You won't be going home to Red Lake this summer. You're going to stay here at Pipestone."

My oldest brother Stanley tells us, "Our mother is still in Sisseton and is ready to have another baby, and nobody got ahold of our family at Red Lake. Now there's nobody to take care of us."

Oh, geez! We want to go home, and all our crying isn't going to change anything. We have to follow orders, and what choice do we have?

In Stink Dormitory we play a game that we call blanket toss. The ceilings in our dormitories are about twelve feet high, so we can really get a blanket toss going. We post a lookout at the door, and the rest of us grab the edges of one of our wool blankets. Then we take turns being thrown up in the air. There's one kid we call Monkey. He can do anything—climb, jump, you name it, he can do it. He's just like a monkey.

Well, one time we're having a blanket toss in Stink Dormitory and it's Monkey's turn. He does all kinds of tricks. He goes right up to the ceiling and hits it with both hands and both feet, and on the way down he does a flip. It's really something to watch, and we're all cheering him on. Everybody's carrying on, all excited about Monkey's flying. We yell, "One, two, three," and toss Monkey up in the air just when the lookout guy at the door hollers, "Mr. Burns is coming!"

Everybody just drops the blanket and runs, and Monkey is going up to the ceiling! The poor guy lands on the hardwood floor instead of the soft blanket. He did recover from that.

‡ ‡ ‡

It seems as though we're always fighting at school. I hate being picked on by big mean boys. Spud Martin is the worst guy. I'm tired of all of them shoving, slapping, punching, and kicking me, and I'm learning to punch back.

Walter Jones laughs when he tells my older brothers what happens to me when they aren't around to defend me. "When a bigger boy punched Adam and made him cry, Adam surprised the big guy and charged at him, screaming and crying. His little arms and fists were going round and round, like a windmill. All it takes is one lucky punch to split the big boy's lip or make his nose bleed, and Adam doesn't have any more trouble from that guy."

We have a lot of bloody noses and black eyes in the boys' dormitory, but nobody wants to be sick at the school. We're most scared of the kind of sickness that spreads around until a whole bunch of kids get sick. When one of us starts to sniffle, pretty soon everybody's got a cold. One guy caught the mumps, and now at least thirty of us guys are sick in bed in the same dormitory. Some of our cheeks are so big and swollen we look like squirrels with cheeks full of acorns. We can't eat regular food, because it's too hard to swallow. So, at each meal older boys who've already had the mumps bring in huge kettles of soup for us. Even that's tough going down.

As the moaning, groaning, and coughing goes on, Roger, in the next bed says, "Adam, you've got to stay warm and keep covered up, or those mumps will go down on you."

"What do you mean, go down on me?"

"If those mumps go down, they go straight to your nuts, and they'll swell up as big as Pat the bull's."

"*Ah waah!* You're just kidding me."

"No, I'm not."

Well, I don't take any chances, and I keep the blankets tucked under my chin for three days. I like my nuts just the way they are. They keep us out of school for two weeks, and that makes all the boys happy.

‡ ‡ ‡

We're doing things different again this Christmas. The teachers are doing a play called "The Little Rich Girl."[5]

Mr. Balmer, our superintendent, is a really nice guy. We've all heard the song called "Auld Lang Syne." It has foreign words to it we can't understand, but we get the melody. Mr. Balmer is on the left side of the stage. The piano player, Mrs. Fisher, a short skinny white woman with dark circles under her eyes, is on the right side, and she starts the melody to "Auld Lang Syne." Mr. Balmer starts singing "Pine tree, pine tree, pine tree," over and over again to the melody. Then he hollers, "All right, you kids, sing along!" Soon three hundred kids, teachers, and school employees are singing "Pine tree, pine tree," to the melody of "Auld Lang Syne." The school auditorium is filled with singing and laughter. You know, the funny thing is that it works!

‡ ‡ ‡

Mr. Balmer says that a lot of people ask what we eat at the school. The staff in home economics, the kitchen, and the bakery make up our menus, and they post them for everyone to see. Here is our holiday season menu:[6]

> *December 24th, Christmas Eve*
> Breakfast: Bananas, krumbles, whole milk, coffee bread, butter, cereal, coffee.
> Dinner: Frankfurters, mashed potatoes, buttered corn, pickles, bread, fruited Jell-O, whole milk.
> Supper: Baked beans, sliced onions, bread, blackberry jam, canned pineapple, lemon cake, whole milk.
> *December 25th, Christmas*
> Breakfast: Grapefruit, oatmeal, whole milk, Swedish tea rings, butter, cocoa.

Dinner: Chicken with wild rice, mashed potatoes, giblet gravy, cranberry mold, fruit salad, sweet pickles, hot rolls, butter, mincemeat pie, whole milk, coffee.

Supper: Vegetable soup, crackers, watermelon pickles, bread, apple butter, loganberries, fruit cake, whole milk.

Other daily menus look like these:

Thursday
Breakfast: Cracked wheat with raisins, brown bread, butter, cereal, whole milk, coffee.

Dinner: Roast beef, brown gravy, steamed potatoes, stewed tomatoes, bread, cornbread, fruit Betty, whole milk.

Supper: Scalloped corn, dill pickles, bread, peanut butter, stewed apricots, cake, hot tea, whole milk.

Friday
Breakfast: Oranges, Rice Krispies, whole milk, raisin rolls, butter, cocoa.

Dinner: Scrambled eggs, mashed potatoes, creamed peas, pear and cheese salad, bread, chocolate blancmange, whole milk.

Supper: Boiled beans, sliced onions, bread, syrup, stewed peaches, peanut butter cookies, whole milk.

Saturday
Breakfast: Stewed prunes, shredded wheat, whole milk, oatmeal, bread, cereal, coffee.

Dinner: Steak with onions, steamed potatoes, buttered string beans, bread, spiced bread pudding, whole milk.

Supper: Meat and vegetable stew, crackers, mustard pickles, bread, mixed dried fruit, whole milk.

‡ ‡ ‡

It's late spring when all the boys and girls go to the hospital for a checkup. One by one, us naked boys go up to Dr. Williams. First he checks my chest with a stethoscope. "Take a deep breath," he says, as he moves the thing across my chest again, and then all around on my back. He looks in both my eyes with a flashlight and says, "We have a lot of trachoma going around the reservations, and we can't be too careful." He checks both my ears with a tiny flashlight.

"Now, open your mouth wide." I do and he puts a flat stick in my mouth and pushes down on my tongue. "Hmm. Hmm."

He turns to the nurse and says, "This boy has enlarged tonsils."

Dang it! The mumps must've gone the wrong way!

Now he pokes around on my stomach with his fingers and asks, "Does it hurt here? Does it hurt here?"

"No, no, no," I answer.

Next, he holds my nuts and says, "Now, cough."

Oh, geez!

A week later a bunch of us boys are checked into the hospital, and they give us short gowns to wear. One by one they take us into the operating room. They put a mask over our nose and mouth and pour ether on it. That knocks us out. When we come to we're in a hospital room, and most of us are as sick as dogs from that ether. We puke into the pans that are next to our beds. After that our throats hurt even worse, because our tonsils have been cut out. The nurses give us some ice cream, and that makes us feel a little bit better.

From my bed I can see the pictures on the walls. Wow! They're all Indians, mostly Blackfeet from Montana, painted by Winold Reiss for the Great Northern Railway calendars. He painted beautiful Indian women, and warriors, and chiefs wearing eagle-feather warbonnets. As soon as we get out of the hospital, more kids come in. This's been going on for three weeks. Now Dr. Williams has cut the tonsils out of seventy boys and girls.[7] Boy, they sure must've used a lot of ice cream.

‡ ‡ ‡

Monkey goes to the Three Maidens, those great big boulders near the sacred quarry. The old Sioux believe the Three Maidens are the mothers of their people. In the cliffs above the pond are kingfishers nesting in the holes. Monkey scrambles up the rocks and reaches into one of the holes and catches a little baby kingfisher. Monkey's really happy, but when he leans back he loses his balance and falls off the cliff. It's a long way down, and he hollers real loud. Some white people visiting the quarry hear his screaming and take him to the hospital. He just keeps on screaming and screaming while they check him all over for anything more serious than bruises. When they can't find anything, they ask him why he's screaming so loud, and he says, "I lost my bird." He's more upset about losing the baby kingfisher than about hitting the ground and getting hurt.[8]

‡ ‡ ‡

It's really hard for Mr. and Mrs. Burns and Paul Smith to keep us boys in line. There're one hundred and fifty of us and only three of them. I think there're times we give them the fits. After the lights go out we raid the boys in the next dorm room. We know they'll want to get back at us, so we booby-trap our room. We prop a broom against a bedstead near the door. When somebody opens that door, that heavy broom falls and the guy that opens the door gets whacked. We make so much noise that Mrs. Burns comes in to check on us. When she opens our door, that heavy broom conks her on the head and almost knocks her down. It looks so funny we want to laugh, but we don't dare.

When she stands up she glares at us with a look that says we are all in real trouble. "Who did that?" she asks. She looks around the room, and we just pull the blankets up to our chins and don't say anything. Nobody wants to be called a "squeal baby."

"Okay, everybody out of your beds and bend over." Wow! That little woman sure knows how to swing that broom, like she's going for a homerun. "*Ow-wah-high! Ow-wah-high!*" (Ouch! That really hurts!)

We aren't about to let a little thing like that stop our dormitory wars. We change our booby traps. Our beds are in rows with walkways between them. When the boys in the next dormitory room start raiding our room, we shove broom handles through the bed frames about a foot off the floor. It's hard to see them in the dark. We just laugh when a boy runs into them. He trips and falls flat on his face. Mr. Burns hears all that noise, and he comes charging into the dormitory swinging his leather strap. Mr. Burns is a big man, and when his shin hits the broom handle, he flies through the air and lands with a loud "whump" on the floor. He's really mad, and he turns on the lights and wants to know who set the trap. Nobody says anything.

"Everybody out of bed and bend over."

Boy! That leather strap sure gets a lot of use tonight. When we catch Paul Smith in the same trap, we get a whipping the same way.

‡ ‡ ‡

This summer we get to go home. Everybody's family and friends meet our bus at the agency. It's a really happy time. Our mom's not here to meet us. We find out that since she's moved to Sisseton, South Dakota, to be with her Sioux husband, she hasn't been in contact with our family, and nobody's made any plans about where to keep us six Nordwall kids. We're stranded on our own reservation!

My older brothers, Stanley and Wally, and my older sister, Myra, all have friends they can stay with. That leaves Curtis, Alton, and me standing here, not knowing where to go or what to do. We're really confused.

The grown-up tribal council members and Bureau of Indian Affairs guys have a quick meeting and decide to send us to a health camp. Before long, we are put on a bus to take us around to the other side of our big lake to Ponemah.

"Ponemah! Oh no!" my brother Curtis is getting upset. Curtis had gone to St. Mary's Catholic school at Red Lake before we all were taken to Pipestone. He tells Alton and me, "Father Simon, Father Florien, and all the nuns told us Ponemah is the home of pagans and heathens that practice devil worship in their Grand Medicine Lodge and in their Medewiwin ceremonies. They told us those people can put curses on you, make bad medicine against you. Now we're going to spend the summer there."

Ho wah!

Mr. Day, the boys' counselor, checks us into the boys' dormitory. It's a lot smaller than Pipestone, and everybody is really friendly to us kids. We even eat like a family with boys, girls, and grown-ups all at the same table.

At ten in the morning, we all line up and the counselors give us a huge spoonful of cod liver oil and an orange. If we want that orange, we have to gulp down that yucky cod liver oil. I'd eat a raw toad to get that tasty orange.

Every day we get to go swimming in the big lake. I don't know how to swim yet, so I just splash around in the shallow water and look at the nice round rocks on the beach.

Once a week we get to see a movie just like in Pipestone. The theater isn't like the big one in Pipestone, it looks more like an old wooden barn. The seats are wood planks that sit on top of wood stumps. Those scary movies give me nightmares.

The camp has a nice woodshop where we can make all kinds of things. They told me the old-time Indians made little boats and filled them with medicine offerings to the lake spirits. After they prayed over them, they'd float those little boats out into the water of the big lake. I want to be like those old-time Indians, so I start to carve a boat out of sugar pine. That sharp chisel slips and cuts a hole clear to the bone of my thumb. After all the accidents I've had at Pipestone, this is no big deal. But I'm sad my little boat never got finished so I could float it on the lake.

Before bedtime is a good time to tell stories. Man alive! Those boys from Ponemah know all kinds of ghost stories about a giant cannibal called Weendigo, flying skeletons, and evil, mean little people that live in the deep woods. Those spooky stories scare the heck out of me, but I still want to hear them.

One morning after our dose of cod liver oil and our orange, Mr. Day announces to us boys, "Today we're going on a nature hike." Here at Ponemah I've seen old things like birch bark wigwams, and the Medewiwin ceremonial grounds, and sweat lodges. Now we have a white guy telling us we're going on a nature walk. Well, okay.

Mr. Day leads a group of about twenty of us boys down the dirt road. Since I'm the smallest, I'm at the end of the line. Alongside the road is a row of small houses all facing the lake. They're so small, they only come up to my belly button.

The Ponemah boys walk on the other side of the road and won't go near those little houses.

"How come?" I ask.

Mr. Day says, "A dead person is buried under each house."

Geez! There could be ghosts all around us! I see little openings cut into the front of each house—moons, stars, and other shapes. Mr. Day says those holes are where family and friends put offerings and medicine gifts for the spirits of the dead.

At Red Lake and Redby, when people die, they're buried in cemeteries and they put markers or tombstones over their graves. Things at Ponemah sure are different.

A little farther down the road, Mr. Day turns off the road and onto a path leading into the deep, dark woods. The path is like a cave going through the forest. The smell of wild mushrooms and rotting stumps makes the air feel heavy. I know the woods are full of bears and wolves, and now I think about all those spirits. Are the dead branches scraping me the bony fingers of the flying skeletons? We go deeper into the dark woods, and I get more afraid of every different sound. A deer crashing though the brush scares me so much that I jump. I'm getting a cold feeling. Something's watching me. I stop and turn around real slow and see two eyes looking at me from the shadow of a tree stump. I get the shivers when I think it might be one of those mean, evil little people. I look real hard at those eyes, and I'm happy to see it's a little woodchuck looking at me.

Whew! I feel so good, I say to the little furry guy, "How much wood could a woodchuck chuck, if a woodchuck could chuck wood?" I've been really scared before, and now saying that stupid little rhyme makes me feel a whole lot better.

I run to catch up to the other boys. They're jumping over a huge log that had fallen across our path. I climb on top of the log, and before I jump to the other side I see something big and round sticking to the log. It isn't anything I know, so I kick it a couple of times. I jump off the log and catch up to the other boys.

In a small clearing at the top of the hill is a real tall fire watchtower. Near it is a small cabin with bearskins nailed to the walls. We all climb the steps clear to the top of the tower, and we can see for miles and miles.

"Time to go back boys," says Mr. Day.

"Ah, geez, do we have to?"

"Yes, we have to get back before supper."

Back on the trail leading to camp, we come to that same big log laying across our path. This time I kick the round grey thing even harder. This time it breaks open. All of a sudden, mad hornets start swarming all over me and they start stinging me. I start screaming and run to catch up to the boys. But they're getting stung by those mad hornets, too. Pretty soon we're all running and screaming through the woods. The stings have swelled my eyes almost shut, and I can't see the boys turn to the right, so I charge straight into a barbed wire fence, the kind with extra long barbs to keep out wild animals. I scream some more, and I pull away from the barbed wire. I feel a tug at my arm. The hornet stings are getting a lot worse.

Mr. Day and the boys get rid of their hornets. They all run over to me and swat those hornets that're all over my body.

"Oh, shit!" Mr. Day is a white man, so I guess it's okay for him to cuss.

He hollers when he sees blood all over my left arm. On my arm by my elbow is a hole torn through the skin. He hurries and wraps my elbow with his handkerchief. He puts me on his back and runs toward camp. When he stops to take a breath, a boy hollers, "Mr. Day, you've got blood running all down your front!"

He turns my arm to the side and sees my wrist is slashed and is squirting blood all over him.

"Oh, damn! Damn!" He tears off his shirttail and wraps my wrist real tight above the cut to slow the bleeding.

By the time we get back to camp my eyes are swollen all the way shut. Welts from the hornet stings are all over my body, and now I'm too weak to cry anymore. Maybe it's because I lost so much blood or it's the poison from the hornets. I don't know.

At the first-aid station they can't use regular stitches to sew me up. They make what they call butterfly stitches out of adhesive tape to pull the torn skin together. Then they wrap my arm in bandages. In less than a week I'm ready for some more cod liver oil and that sweet orange.

‡ ‡ ‡

It's kind of sad when summer ends when I'm having so much fun. We're loaded on a bus to take us back to the agency at Red Lake. They tell Curtis, Alton, and me to wait there for the bus to Pipestone. An Indian employee of the agency looks us over and says, "You boys can't go to school looking like that."

We hadn't thought about that. Our clothes are rags and our shoes are worn out. He takes us to the commissary and gives us new coveralls and new shoes,

all three or four sizes too big. Alton and I sit on the rear porch of the maintenance shop and cry our eyes out.

When the bus comes I'm still crying. I sit next to Calvin Iceman. He's got a
big sack of hazelnuts, and he gives me some. He knows I can't eat and cry at
the same time.

‡ ‡ ‡

I've met a new kid at school. We're both in Miss Carvella's fourth grade
class. His name is Joe Crown, a Chippewa from Onegum on the Leech Lake
Indian Reservation. Now we're really good friends.

After we finish our chores, four of us boys sit at one of the tables in the
basement where we get our bug rake checks. Three of us are from Red Lake,
plus Joe Crown. The fingertips of his right hand are kinda funny.

"How come your hand's like that?" I ask.

Joe starts telling us a story, and it almost makes me cry. When he was four
years old his father and uncles had gone out deer hunting. An Indian agent,
two missionaries, and Father Simon and Father Causian showed up at his little tarpaper shack at Onegum and took him away. His mother was screaming
and crying as they loaded Joe into a car for a trip to a place he'd never been—
a place called St. Mary's Mission School on the Red Lake Indian Reservation.
Sister Laura checked little Joe into the girls' dormitory.

The next day Joe's father and uncles showed up saying they wanted to take
Joe back home. Sister Laura wouldn't let them see Joe, and they were turned
away by Father Simon.

A bunch of other boys come to the table to listen.

Joe said that then he could understand only a few words of English and
mostly spoke Chippewa. When he spoke Chippewa at the mission school, a
nun would whack him across his fingers. When he asked why, the nuns told
him, "Your language is the language of the heathens and savages. Your language is the language of the devil!"

Some of the other boys at the table agree, "Yup, Joe's right about the mission
school."[9]

The next time Sister Laura caught Joe talking Chippewa she grabbed him by his ear, pulled him down the hallway, out the back door, and down to the root cellar. The root cellar didn't have any windows, and so it was cold and dark all the time. She swung open the big door and threw Joe down the steps, and he started screaming. Joe turned around and put up his hands to stop the heavy door from slamming shut. The tips of his fingers were smashed in the doorjamb.

Joe's story gets a boy from Red Lake talking. Clifford Red Thunder says, "Hey! Did you know that mean Father Causian is a drunk? Every Saturday night he goes to Redby for a drinking party. He plays poker with all the local lumber mill workers. Every Sunday morning they take two girls from the mission school out there to clean up the mess. Father Causian leads Sunday morning Mass, and when he gets to preaching at us Indians he tells us how evil our ways are: our ceremonies, our dancing, our language. He rants and raves about the evil of drinking alcohol, and all the time he's hanging onto the pulpit with a big hangover."

All us boys laugh.

Clifford goes on with his story. "Last year Father Causian saw two boys walking down the hallway. One was talking Chippewa to the other. Father Causian got really mad. He took the boy into his office, ripped off his shirt, and bent him over his desk. Then Father Causian grabbed a buggy whip and lashed that boy until he had bloody welts all over his back."

The rest of us boys don't know what to say, because it's so awful.

Clifford says, "The two boys got away from the mission school and ran to the boys' grandfather's. After hearing the boys' story their grandfather called relatives, the elders, and the district chief to a meeting to tell about what happened to the boys. Father Causian was called in and he claimed he did nothing wrong, and that he was only doing his Christian duty and was beating the devil out of that boy.

"The grandfather then took the shirt off his grandson, and showed the scabby welts on his back. The chief got mad and yelled at Father Causian, 'You get the goddamn hell out of here! Get off our reservation! Never come back! You are banished!'"

All the boys around the table cheer.

Then Joe Crown asks, "Do they punish you for speaking your language here at this school?"

"No, never," says another boy from Red Lake. "I've been here four years, and I've never seen anybody punished for that. I speak Chippewa and have seen Sioux boys sitting in a circle on the lawn or sitting on the pipe railing next to the road speaking Sioux. Nobody's ever stopped them or punished them."

Even though we never see anybody punished for speaking their tribal language, there is one language that is strictly forbidden. They call it cussing. If Mr. or Mrs. Burns catches any boy cussing they will wash his mouth out with soap. For the worst cussing he gets a spanking. When they warn us to "Watch your language," they don't mean our tribes' languages. Even at home my mother says we don't cuss or use that kind of language. In fact, she said the old-time Indians never used cuss words. They would insult somebody, but they didn't cuss at them. Here at school we insult each other—the Sioux boys call us Chippewas "rabbit chokers" and we call them "dog eaters."

Somebody in the crowd yells, "Hey, Clifford, can you tell us more stories about St. Mary's?"

He shakes his head and says, "Nah! I've probably said too much already. I could get in real trouble back home."

Joe Crown says, "Yeah, I know what you mean. We should be fair with that mission school, because Father Florien is a really good guy. He's always helping Indian people, not just at Red Lake, but at White Earth and Leech Lake, too. He really tries to understand us. And most of the nuns are really nice too."

The Red Lake boys make a list and rate the priests of St. Mary's Mission School. Father Florian, he's a good guy. Father Simon is a mean guy. Both Fathers Thomas and Benno learned the Chippewa language and are good guys. Father Egbert is a mean guy who likes to whip the boys. Father Causian is mean and is an alcoholic.

Joe Crown finishes by saying, "Compared to the mission school, Pipestone is a little bit of heaven."

‡ ‡ ‡

Not only are we punished for cussing, but if we get caught smoking, we quickly feel the sting of a leather strap or belt. The bigger boys that want to act grown up pick up cigarette butts in town from ashtrays and off sidewalks. They sneak smokes behind the big brick incinerator behind the boys' dormitory. Joe Crown, Sugar Mahto, and I are shooting a game of marbles, and one of the older boys comes over to tell us some awful news. He says his friend Norbert, one of the oldest boys in school, got hooked on smoking cigarettes. He's always mooching cigarettes or smoking butts he finds on the ground. He's smoked so much his teeth are yellow, his fingers are yellow, and even his fingernails turned yellow. He got sick and they took him to the boarding school hospital, and Dr. Williams said Norbert was suffering from nicotine poisoning.

"*Ah waah!*" The boys cry. "We don't believe you!"

"Yeah, it's true," says the older boy. "They wrapped Norbert in clean sheets and put him in a sweat box, a steam box, and it was really hot. Norbert started sweating real good. He sweated so much, those clean white sheets turned yellow from the nicotine. They sweated him for a week, and before they checked him out, he told me that if he ever catches any of you little boys smoking, he's going to beat the crap out of you!"

Now, I've been beat up a lot of times by bigger boys. Black eyes, a bloody nose, or fat lips are nothing new to me. I just don't want them to have any excuse to beat me up, so I tell Joe and Sugar, "I'm never, ever, going to smoke cigarettes. But if I do, I'm going to smoke Camels because they advertise 'less nicotine.'"

‡ ‡ ‡

We wake up real early from a boy shouting, "There's a blizzard outside." The windows of the dormitory are rattling from the wind whistling through the cracks. We hurry up and get dressed and make our beds.

Some of us are real happy, and we go down to the landing that goes to the lavatory. It has doors to the outside on both sides. It's just like a football rally with all the cheering. One boy strips off all his clothes. Somebody opens the door, and he runs out into the freezing storm. A little while later there's pounding on the other door. We let in a happy kid that's just run naked around the boys' dormitory. He has snowflakes stuck all over him, and his teeth are chattering like crazy. He puts on his long-john wool underwear with a flap in the back, but before he finishes dressing three or four other boys and I strip off our clothes and head out the door, yelling and laughing as we go. We all cheer when all us boys come back safe and sound. It takes me a half an hour to thaw out.

One of the boys asks, "What if somebody saw us?"

"If anybody sees naked Indian boys running around in a freezing snow blizzard, who'd believe them?"

That big blizzard's roared right on into the weekend. There aren't that many trees on the prairie to slow down the wind, so it screams and howls through the boarding school. Saturday morning we have to change all the sheets in the boys' dormitory. The beds are stripped and the sheets are put into pillowcases, and a pile of pillowcases are tied into a bundle like Santa Claus's. Getting those bundles to the laundry behind the girls' dormitory is going to be tough with the wind and snow blowing so hard.

Ten of us boys are on laundry duty. We all troop out of the dormitory with big bundles over our shoulders. The southwest corner of the building is like a windbreak, so we all stop there to figure out what to do next. We have to cross that awful windy road to the shelter of the next buildings, then it's not so bad the rest of the way to the laundry.

"You go first!"

"No! You go first!"

Nobody wants to be the first one to cross that windy road because the storm's really howling and the snow's flying sideways and we can barely see through it.

Finally Sugar Mahto yells, "I'll go!" He takes off running with a big bundle on his back. He looks like a crazy elf. Halfway across the road a blast of wind opens his bundle and all the sheets blow out. He tries to hang on and the bundle turns into a parachute, and the strong wind picks up Sugar like a rag doll and carries him a hundred and fifty feet. He falls on the road next to the totem pole. The rest of us boys throw our bundles into the corner of the building and

Clagne Hall, our new school building, and totem pole carved by the boys. Courtesy Pipestone County Historical Society, Pipestone, Minnesota.

run down to help Sugar. He isn't hurt at all. In fact, he's laughing because he's never had a ride like that in his life. We figure that after that, Sugar Mahto has to be the boarding school's first paratrooper.

The storm's over and so's the fun. Most of us boys have to clean the snow off the sidewalks and steps.

We have a brand new power plant to heat the school. The guys used to shovel the coal into the old one's big furnaces. The new one has a chute that the coal goes through down into the furnaces. They put all the steam pipes and hot water pipes in the tunnels under the main sidewalks of the school. I found that out the hard way when I fell through an open manhole onto those asbestos-covered pipes. The big cut I got on my chin healed pretty fast.

The hot pipes are covered with asbestos sleeves that're three feet long and are held in place with tin strips and wire buckles. Those warm sidewalks melt off the snow, but there are a lot of other sidewalks that we have to shovel. The roads around the school and the one leading to town are all cleared by snowplows. We've made a snow pile six-feet high in front of the administration building. It's so big we have to play on it. We've dug snow caves all through it. When we finish shoveling and playing in the snow we all go into the basement to warm up. The steam pipes coming into the north side of the basement are all wrapped in asbestos sleeves, and the boys can lay on them to warm up without getting burned. We take off the tin straps of some of the higher pipes so we can get those asbestos sleeves. They make great bats. Everybody's grabbing half a sleeve, and we all start whacking each other like we're having a big pillow fight. We're all laughing, and parts of the sleeves are flying all over the basement. It's so much fun.

Paul Smith, the assistant boys' advisor, is the party pooper. "All right you boys, clean up this mess."

"Gee whiz, Mr. Smith, we're just having fun."

‡ ‡ ‡

Our school has a gym made of creamy yellow brick. It must have everything. It's got toilets, showers, and high bleachers on both sides of the floor. There's a double-door entryway, and on one wall of it is a bulletin board and next to that is a big poster of the Fred Waring and His Pennsylvanians orchestra.

The floor is made of tongue-in-groove hardwood. Four of us boys can have the entire floor waxed and polished in half an hour. We use a big electric floor buffer and wide push brooms with cloth instead of bristles that we put O-Cedar floor polish on. Sweeping the bleachers is a lot tougher. Every time the gym's used we have to clean the whole thing, and that means the bathrooms, too.

‡ ‡ ‡

After the hard freezes of winter set in, teams of men go to Indian lakes that are just below the boarding school. They've got all kinds of tools like huge ice saws with big sharp teeth. We watch the men cut rows of ice blocks and then drag them to the snowy pond banks. They load all those ice blocks on trucks and take them to icehouses next to the railroad tracks. Just like loading hay into our barn lofts, those blocks of ice are hoisted into the icehouse, and then each layer is covered with sawdust. They put in layer after layer, until the icehouse is full. They use that ice to keep food in the boxcars cool. The ice is used to keep the iceboxes cool around town and at the boarding school, too. Electric refrigerators are too expensive for most people, so they just keep their food cool in old-fashioned iceboxes.

The night before the iceman comes to the school, we put a little sign in the window. It has numbers on it, and a red arrow points to how many pounds of ice we need that day. When the ice truck shows up at school, the iceman figures out how much ice we want, then he breaks off the right size block with his ice pick. He picks up the ice block with ice tongs, and he swings the block of ice up onto his shoulder and carries it inside to our icebox. Almost every time the ice truck shows up, it's followed by a group of us boys picking up and eating the pieces of chipped-off ice.

We sit and watch all the work at the icehouse. Edsel Esty, one of our older boys, sees something different. If he can climb up that pulley rope to the top of the ice tower, he can get into the warehouse. That's where so many good things are stored, like beer.

It doesn't take long for Edsel to get six young warriors to stage a raid on that big fort of a warehouse. After Friday night bed check, Edsel and his friends sneak out of the dormitory and across the grounds to the railroad tracks that go directly to town.

Once the little band of boys get to the warehouse, Edsel grabs the pulley rope and climbs all the way to the top of the icehouse. He lets himself inside the little door that we saw the blocks of ice go through.

A door on the ground floor slowly opens, and Edsel waves the boys inside. They're all really quiet. They go in and, just as quiet, they come out. Each one is carrying a case of beer. They sneak down to the quarries, a half a mile away, and hide the beer in the creek to keep it cold. Then they have a quiet little beer party every night that lasts two weeks. Edsel doesn't want the boys to drink too much beer, so he only lets each of us have one bottle a night, just enough so we stagger. Nobody at the school knows what's going on until somebody sees Billy Fairbanks sitting on top of the root cellar drinking the last of the beer in his bottle. He loses his balance and rolls down the slope of the root cellar and laughs all the way. Mr. Burns picks up the empty beer bottle and can't figure out how Billy got the beer. The other boys have been throwing their empty bottles in the creek. Nobody'll find them there.

‡ ‡ ‡

I love to listen to the older boys tell stories. They come from different tribes: Sioux, Omaha, Winnebago, Oneida, and Chippewa. They really try to scare the heck out of me, but the stories like the coyote stories make me laugh because they can be so stupid. The boys tell stories about warriors and great brave chiefs. A lot of times they faced death to save their people.

"Why do you think we play our warrior games here at school?" asks Clifford Crooks. "You never know. Someday we might have to be warriors."

We all go to the basement to choose sides. Joe Bebeau and Spud Martin pick their warriors. Joe Crown and I pick our team. We have a five-minute head start to hide anywhere we want, all over the school grounds. We are playing hide-and-seek, only really rough. When Joe Bebeau's warriors catch one of us we're their prisoner, and they hide him and wait for our guys to rescue him. They catch Dopey Sayers and take him to a road grader. Joe Bebeau and Spud Martin turn the huge control wheels and raise the steel blade. They put Dopey under the blade and crank the wheels and lower the blade against Dopey's belly. They pin him to the ground.

Joe Crown finds out that I'm missing. The enemy grabs me behind the horse barn, takes me inside, and ties me flat on my back to a plank between the haylofts. Below me are those big Belgian workhorses. They're snorting because they don't know what's going on. Spud Martin finds a handsaw and saws on the end of the plank until I hear it start to break. He tells me, "Adam, if you move, you're gonna break that plank and fall to the horse stalls below you. Those big horses will stomp you into the floor like horse shit!" I remember going to the Saturday matinee in town and seeing *The Perils of Pauline*. The bad guy ties the beautiful girl to the train tracks, and the big black train is coming straight at her. "Hey, somebody help me!"

Joe Crown hears me calling from inside the barn. I hear the boys coming for me, and I holler out a warning about the cut plank. I don't dare move. The boys bring another good plank and shove it alongside of me, and roll me over onto it. They untie me, and I can see those big horses milling around below me. Wow! That's a close call!

The weather's getting colder and colder, and we can hear Dopey screaming. We find him and turn those steel wheels and lift that big blade off his belly.

We all go back to the basement, where it's Joe's and Spud's team's turn to hide and our team are the hunters.

We wait five minutes, and then we go outside to start hunting and the snow is really flying. Our team spreads out to check every kind of hiding place on the school grounds. Three of our guys catch Spud Martin behind the water tower. They open the manhole cover with a steel hinge at the bottom of the tower. There's a steel ladder that goes down to the big main water valves. Spud Martin has to climb down that ladder, and they shut the manhole cover down over him with a clang. His team's going to have a heck of a time finding him. Now, we've got more guys to help us find Joe Bebeau. It's really snowing a lot, and it's so deep it's making it really tough to walk around and find anybody. We finally find Joe Bebeau hiding behind one of the brick columns at the entrance to the school. We put his back to a telephone pole and chain his arms behind him. Just for good measure, we put a gag in his mouth to keep him from yelling for help. We leave him alone in the snowstorm.

Our team runs back to the basement to wait for Joe Bebeau's team to rescue our captives. We've captured and hidden their leaders, and the rest of the boys have a heck of a time finding everybody else. Spud Martin finds a wrench on the floor and pounds on the manhole cover with it. His team hears that clanging sound, and they find and rescue him.

In the basement everybody is waiting to see who's found. Everybody is here but Joe Bebeau. His team sends out one group after another to find him, but they come back empty-handed. Finally, Spud Martin says to Joe Crown, "Okay. We give up. Where is he?"

Hospital and brick column at entrance to school grounds. Courtesy Pipestone County Historical Society, Pipestone, Minnesota.

All of us head out of the basement to the school entrance. Joe Bebeau's still there all covered with snow. His teeth are chattering, and he's turning kinda blue. We take out his gag and undo the chains. He can barely stand up, so we help him back to the basement to thaw out.

You know, that guy's really tough! If you're going to be a warrior, you gotta be tough.

‡ ‡ ‡

I really like working on the bakery detail because we're always hungry. The food we make in our kitchen never does taste so good, since most of it's steamed in huge pots or boiled with nothing added. When Mrs. Trottachaud was the baker she had a crew of eight girls to do the work. When Mr. Bushyhead took over the girls were replaced by boys, and that's okay with me.

We have to bake enough bread for three meals every day for three hundred kids. I think our baker's outfit is pretty nice. We wear white pants, white T-shirts, a white apron, and a little white cap. Mr. Bushyhead says we have to wear clean, white clothes to dress the part, and we have to stay clean. He's teaching us how to read the recipes and how to use all the machines. The bread-dough mixer is a monster, and it has paddle-like blades that mix the dough. We take that dough out of the mixer and put it on a long work table that has flour on it. We roll and cut the dough into one-pound sections, and then they go into big baking pans, five loaves at a time. We roll racks of bread dough into a big warmer so the dough can rise. Then we put them in a two-level oven to bake until they're golden brown. As soon as the loaves come out of the oven, we rub butter on the crusts.

Boy! That fresh-baked bread sure smells good. I'm learning how to be a really good baker. Mr. Bushyhead's teaching me how to bake bread, pies, cinnamon rolls, upside-down cake, and, best of all, devil's food cake. My cakes turn out so moist and delicious, even the school employees come to the bakery looking for some. Now I bake an extra pan of devil's food cake just for them.

Mr. Bushyhead says, "Adam, today you're going to bake oatmeal cookies."

Wow! I love oatmeal cookies. I follow the recipe, mix the dough, and spoon it onto big, flat pans.

I guess cookies bake a lot faster than bread. I burned two whole pans. Mr. Bushyhead tells me, "Throw them out!"

Even if the cookies are burnt I think the boys can still eat them. On the way to the garbage cans on the porch, I see a bunch of boys coming back from garden detail.

"Snatch grab! Snatch grab!" I holler, and I start tossing those big oatmeal cookies to the boys. All the boys get really excited and start yelling and jumping and grabbing those flying cookies. Billy Fairbanks jumps too high, and a big burnt cookie whacks him right on the nose. He's got a bloody nose, and he's crying and cussing at the same time. He yells that I broke his nose.

"Shut up! Forget the blood and eat your cookie," I yell back.

Making bread rolls is fun, and Mr. Bushyhead is showing us how to roll out the dough into long, kinda thick strips. Then we cut them into two-inch lengths. We put those chunks of dough on a table covered with flour. We use both hands to roll those chunks into round dough balls, and then we put them into a baking pan. We're making two rolls at the same time—one in each hand—and we're all getting really fast at it.

After we're done baking we have to clean up all the messy pots, pans, kettles, and all the machines. I clean out that giant mixer by scraping off all the

Girls in bakery. Courtesy Pipestone County Historical Society, Pipestone, Minnesota.

dough I can get at. I push the start button just enough to turn the big blades a little bit, scrape off as much as I can, and then push the button again. I stick my hand into the machine before the big blades stop. When they do stop, they're right on top of my fingers. I try to pull my hand out but I'm caught in a big mousetrap. Mr. Bushyhead and the boys all come over to help me out. They pull the blades just enough to free my hand. My Bushyhead says, "Adam, you're darn lucky those blades didn't go any further, because they'd cut off all your fingers. Next time be patient and wait for those blades to stop."

After we clean up the bakery, Mr. Bushyhead goes to the bulletin board and reads the week's menu and circles all the things we need to bake for the next meals. A lot of the menu looks better on paper than it does on our plates.

I read a notice at the bottom of the menu on the bulletin board: "Leftover food served with evening meals. Whole milk served at all meals. In the middle of the morning and again in the afternoon all first graders and undernourished children are given a bowl of milk. It is of interest, also, that all of such little children are taken to the dormitories immediately after dinner for an hour's rest period before resuming their studies."[10]

I ask Mr. Bushyhead, "What does 'undernourished' mean?"

"When we get some poor kids from the reservation they are suffering from malnutrition, which is a little way from starvation. They don't get much and mostly eat lard sandwiches."

"When I'm at Grandma and Grandpa's place we always get lard sandwiches."

"Yes, but you also eat other food like deer meat, fish, and vegetables, ̵

"Oh, yeah, we eat all kinds of stuff."

Well, Mr. Bushyhead tells me those other kids aren't so lucky. All the ̵ ̵ ̵ ̵ ̵ is lard sandwiches. That's why they come here undernourished.

At Red Lake a little girl died. A group of men sit on a wooden bench in front of Fairbank's store and talk about the little girl's death. The father overhears the conversation and gets really mad. He says, "My little girl didn't starve to death. I looked at the death certificate, and where it says 'cause of death' it says 'mal-new-trish-on'!"

‡ ‡ ‡

Here at the boarding school, the boys can always find a way to get into trouble and the girls are no different. A bunch of girls are supposed to clean and straighten up the big basement storeroom under the dining hall and kitchen. There are all kinds of boxes and barrels that're filled with kitchen supplies. The shelves are full of the canned foods they fixed last summer. When Evelyn Porter and Josephine Smith open a barrel of vinegar, those two tough girls decide to make home brew. The basement lights are kinda dim, and a box they think is full of soda is something called sodium fluoride, a poison we use to kill cockroaches. They mix up some beer, and thirteen girls drink that yucky stuff. When the poison gets ahold of those girls they all start getting sick and vomiting. They run screaming and crying back to the girls' dormitory. My sister Myra says a couple of those girls don't want Miss Freeman to know they're sick, so they're hiding in the closets.

School staff are rounding up the sick girls and taking them to the boarding school hospital. Ten-year-old Bernice Keezer dies there. The rest of the girls have awful stomach aches, but they're all supposed to live.[11]

Mr. Herman Trottachaud is driving Bernice's body more than two hundred and fifty miles to her home village, Waubun, on the White Earth Reservation. William Keezer is burying Bernice next to her mother. Mr. Keezer now has only four kids at the boarding school.

‡ ‡ ‡

They call our school Pipestone Indian Training School for a good reason. They train us. They teach us so many different things. In the classrooms they teach us reading, writing, and arithmetic. For me the best time of all is after school, when I get to go on work details. I especially like the carpentry shop. In the carpentry shop we learn how to take care of the school. Mr. Caulkins runs the shop and is a funny little man who knows a lot about his kind of work.

A leak in the roof of the hospital made part of the plaster ceiling fall down. Mr. Caulkins and five of us boys go to the hospital, where he shows us how to mix plaster. He goes up a ladder, and he covers the broken area with runny plaster from his hod. He's about to come down the ladder, and the whole load of wet plaster falls on his bald head. Mr. Caulkins squeals as loud as the pigs being butchered in the pigpen. He glares at us boys, and we don't dare smile. The next time the plaster isn't so wet, and it holds onto the ceiling.

Upstairs from the carpentry shop is the woodworking shop. Mr. Sid Browdell is the shop instructor. He's more quiet and fun than Mr. Caulkins. Mr. Browdell's teaching us all kinds of woodworking skills, tinsmithing, and copper work. Mr. Browdell has a kinda cage-like office, and he locks up all the small tools there. His shop has everything except a bathroom. Mr. Browdell keeps a small bucket by the window for him to use. Mr. Caulkins is downstairs in the carpentry shop sweeping up a pile of wood shavings. Upstairs Mr. Browdell hears nature's call and fills his little bucket and throws it out the window, right when Mr. Caulkins is on the porch emptying the pile of wood shavings. We can hear Mr. Caulkins's screeching howls and cuss words over all the machines. Everybody in the carpentry shop stops moving. We peek out the windows in time to see Mr. Caulkins dripping from Mr. Browdell's pee.

We heard Mr. Browdell's family has a big ranch in Texas, and they struck big oil. He and his family are millionaires overnight. Mr. Burns tells me that Mr. Browdell quit his job at Pipestone and moved to a big mansion in Texas, and just for old times' sake he keeps a pee bucket by the window.

"*Ah waah!* Mr. Burns, you're just pulling my leg." It seems as though everybody at Pipestone is a storyteller.

Even though I'm in the lower grades I'm being taught how to glaze a window, how to cut the glass, and how to put in the putty. Mr. Caulkins shows me

Boys' carpentry shop, ca. 1930. Courtesy Pipestone County Historical Society, Pipestone, Minnesota.

how to get the putty ready by mixing it with linseed oil and kneading it just like bread dough until it gets soft enough to use. I see that the wood cabinet where we store the putty is always full of mouse crap.

I ask, "How come?"

Mr. Caulkins tells me that the mice love to eat the putty because they like the linseed oil. "They eat and crap, eat and crap, all night long." It's amazing what I'm learning in school.

‡ ‡ ‡

We go to the city dump at Pipestone to get what we need to make toys. Almost everything can be used. We cut old rubber inner tubes into slingshots. A roller skate gets a handle and a seat and turns into a scooter. We even learn how to make boomerangs. They're like crazy flying bats. We don't know where the heck they're going, and we have to run and duck from those chunks of wood. That's a lot of fun.

Making bows and arrows is easy, and when George Skye is showing off his new bow and arrows at the football field he shoots an arrow straight up to show how high it can go. That arrow comes straight down and puts his right eye out.

‡ ‡ ‡

When the soles on my shoes wear out, I go to a corner area of the carpentry shop to the big slabs of cowhide that hang on the wall. I cut a chunk of cowhide and soak it in a big bucket of water to soften it up. Then, I trace the outline of my shoe on the leather and cut out a half sole. I put my shoe on a metal shoe-tree on a tall iron stand, and I nail the half sole to my shoe and trim the cowhide to fit my shoe. I put on new rubber heels, and my shoes are done. I can always tell a boy with new half soles and heels, because he looks an inch taller and goes clump, clump, clump down the hallway, kinda like Frankenstein in the scary movie wearing those shoes with thick soles.

Putting those half soles on our shoes has made a problem. Those little nails on the inside that we can't flatten by pounding on them on the shoetree are really sharp and tear up our socks.

Mrs. Burns has seen all our holey socks in the laundry, and she's piled them on a table in our clothing room. She's ordered ten of us boys to sit down, and we're going to get a lesson in darning. I complain that, "Boys don't do darning; that's girls' work." She whacks me two times with a leather strap and convinces me that I'm going to learn how to darn. She gives us each a lightbulb, needle, and darning thread. Mrs. Burns shows us how to shove the lightbulb into the neck of the sock.

"Stitch side-to-side one way, now weave side-to-side the other way." It's kinda fun, and it doesn't take us long to darn all the holey socks on the table. Since we always make holes in our socks, Mrs. Burns keeps on teaching other boys how to darn socks. We don't dare tell the girls that the boys know how to darn socks or mend our own clothes. They would just cover their mouths and giggle.

‡ ‡ ‡

"If boys can fight, boys can box!" says Superintendent Balmer. He's organized a boxing team, and Paul Smith is going to be the coach. Paul recruits the toughest, strongest boys. Nobody wants to fight Clarence Crooks because he's a southpaw. Joe Crown, Spud Martin, Sugar Mahto, my brother Curtis, and a couple others sign up, too. They've set up boxing matches in nearby towns: Luverne, Worthington, Flandreau, and Pipestone. Our boys are darn good boxers and win most of their fights.

"Hey, Adam!" It's Joe Crown. "We're going to fight Pipestone next week. Wanna join us?"

I know Mr. Balmer's really proud of his boxing team and treats them to a big meal at the Eagle Cafe in Pipestone after the fights. I don't care if my opponent knocks me on my butt. It'll be worth it for a real restaurant dinner.

We're all in the dressing room at the Pipestone gym getting ready for the boxing matches, when the boy who's supposed to fight me comes in to check me out. Instead of a smile and a handshake, I give him my best "mad dog" look. That kid goes out the door looking scared. When our fight's called he never shows up, and I win without even throwing a punch. The victory meal at the Eagle Cafe tastes extra good. The other boys earned their meal, but I haven't even broken a sweat. I decide to quit the boxing team and claim I'm an undefeated champion, and I never had to throw a punch.

‡‡‡

We don't get to go home this summer because there's nobody to take care of us. Since school let out Mr. Burns has doubled up on our work details. And boy, there's a lot to do.

Sugar Mahto, Clifford Crooks, me, and a bunch of other boys are on the lawn detail. There're twelve of us boys all together. Mr. Caulkins takes out the lawnmowers he keeps under the stairway that goes up to the wood shop. We are all busy scraping, cleaning, and oiling the lawnmowers. Mr. Caulkins sharpens the blades and shows us how to adjust the cutting edge of the blades for a good, clean cut.

That darn grass, from springtime till fall, it never quits growing. We mow every lawn on the school grounds and the football field. Pushing those lawnmowers is a real tough job. Day after day, all summer long, our crew cuts the grass. And now, a funny kind of thing is happening. All us little skinny boys are growing muscles. *Ho wah!* After a shower we look in the mirror and flex our muscles. Little, scrawny arms are now getting strong.

"Well, boys," says Mr. Caulkins, "it's time to mow the football field again." It's the middle of summer and it's real hot and sticky. We line up our lawnmowers on the field, one behind the other at an angle, so we can cut twelve feet at a time. Round and round we go, mowing that big field. When we finish, we push our mowers back to the carpentry shop. We are all sweating like heck, and we all lay down on the lawn in front of the boys' dormitory. The tree shade feels so good, and most of us boys fall asleep for a nap.

"Hey, Clifford!" I poke Clifford Crooks laying next to me. "What the heck is that?" I point to a boy laying flat on his back. His mouth is wide open, and flies are going in and out of his mouth, nose, and ears.

"Something's wrong!"

A couple of us haul the boy to the hospital. We wait a few minutes, and then they tell us, "The boy is dead." He's a new kid and I don't even know his name, and we don't know how or why he died.

‡ ‡ ‡

This summer my brother Alton is picked to be on the evening milking crew for his work detail. At the end of the first week Mr. Brush and Charley Morrison get the boys together in the dairy. Charley brings in loaves of bread and breaks them in halves and hollows them out. From the freezer Mr. Brush grabs a tall can full of homemade vanilla ice cream. The boys get in line and Mr. Brush scoops out the ice cream and fills the hollowed-out bread. The boys immediately start to lick and slurp the ice cream before it has a chance to melt—all the boys but Alton.

I'm sound asleep in Dormitory Seven and I feel someone gently shaking my shoulder. It's my brother Al. "You want some ice cream?" he asks.

I must be dreaming! But this is a great dream. I sit up in bed and start eating that delicious, creamy ice cream. The other boys in the next beds wake up, and Alton passes around the ice cream until it's all gone. Just as quietly as he came in, he slips out of our dormitory, down the hall, and up the long stairs to his own dormitory room.

‡ ‡ ‡

During the summer we get a lot of time to play and have adventures.

Joe Bebeau knows we are losing our old-time ways, and on Saturday he rounds up a small group of boys to go on a hike to the city dump two miles

Alton Nordwall wears watch chain, but no watch, 1941. Author's collection.

away. Joe shows us how old-time warriors and hunters would dogtrot. It's an easy trot, and he makes us do it all day. "Be sure and keep your toes pointed forward, straight in line with the direction you are going. The white man has his toes off to the side; that's why it's easy to track 'em." Off we go, eight little Indian boys. We dogtrot off the boarding school grounds, across the railroad tracks, and head southwest across the rolling prairie. About a half mile away from the city dump we dogtrot across a farmer's field full of big fat chickens. We get to eat chicken only three times a year: Thanksgiving, Christmas, and New Year's. Joe Bebeau pretends he's ignoring the chickens, and we dogtrot past the farm to the city dump. We scrounge up long poles, mop handles, and broom handles. We find steel spikes and other long skinny pieces of metal. We all make our own spears.

Dogtrotting back to the boarding school, us boys look like a war party carrying our long deadly spears. The flock of chickens now looks like a herd of big buffaloes. With war whoops and hollers, we charge the herd of buffalo chickens. We spear one when it tries to squeeze through the fence. We pretend we're warriors one hundred years ago, killing buffalo on the prairie. We go back to the parching place behind the school. The parching place is kinda hidden by little trees and a row of wild plum bushes. The stone fireplaces are at the bottom of two huge pits that're twenty feet across and four feet deep. We cook our chicken and parch some corn. It doesn't matter that the chicken is burnt on the outside and raw on the inside. It's something we did ourselves. We go back to school, round the corner of the gymnasium, and are stopped by Mrs. Burns. And she is really mad. She has a long, leather strap, and she makes us stand in a line and she sits on the steps of the gym. One by one, we bend over her knees and she whacks the hell out of our little butts. As his turn to get a whipping comes up, Dopey starts crying out, "I didn't kill that chicken! I didn't kill that chicken!"

Mrs. Burns asks, "What chicken?"

Dopey has spilled the beans. Mrs. Burns is punishing us for missing our Saturday showers and clean clothes. Now we have to stand in line again for a second whipping. Most of the boys are crying, but not Joe Bebeau. He takes the whipping in silence. Warriors don't cry.

‡ ‡ ‡

It's after bed check, and Joe Crown shakes me awake. "Get up, Adam. We're going to Beede's Bakery."

I hurry and slip out the back door of the dormitory. We stay in the dark spots so nobody can see us. When we get to the school entrance, we start dogtrotting to town a mile and a half away. When we trot into town we take the back alley that leads us straight to Beede's Bakery. There's a little shed in the back of the bakery that they put the day-old stuff in. There isn't a lock on the door, just a handle. We help ourselves to old pies, cakes, cookies, and sweet rolls. We talk and laugh quietly as we grab some loot and head back to the boarding school. We have a quiet little party with the other boys in the dormitory.

‡ ‡ ‡

"C'mon, Adam, let's go to the quarries," says Clifford Crooks. He is a year older than me, and he has two of his brothers and some other boys with him. The quarries are only about a half-mile away from the school. Ever since I've been old enough, I like to go to look at the falls and play. The quarries are just a little way downstream from the falls.

On the prairie near the quarry is a nice white canvas tent. Amos Crooks has a big smile on his face when he sees his sons.

Clifford told me his mother, Ellen, died in 1936 and left seven boys and two girls. That left Amos stuck with too many kids to take care of. But now Amos has no choice, so all his kids go to the boarding schools. Clifford's story sounds a lot like my own family's story.

I look around and I see other tents set up near the quarries. I meet all the people that live there during the summer: George Bryan and his wife Clara, the Taylors, the Montgomerys, the Derbys. All of them are nice to us kids, who hang around their camps like a pack of dogs looking for handouts.

All of Amos's boys help him dig the stone that's under ten feet of hard rock. That pipestone is blood red and is soft enough to cut with a handsaw.

George Bryan, a Chippewa guy, has his pit on the north side of the rock dam. I sit on the edge of the pit and watch the men and women working. The women sit there holding big chisels against the hard rock. George Bryan and his brother-in-law hit those chisels with sledgehammers. I would be scared as heck if I held one of those chisels, but those women just talk away. The men say they call that gossip. I tell them I think that gossip means women's talk. They all laugh.

At lunchtime Amos invites me to eat with him and the boys. Amos gives me something we never get at the boarding school. Clifford calls it mush melon, but Amos calls it cantaloupe. I don't care what they call it 'cause it tastes really good. It's full of tiny little seeds that Amos throws out in the grass, and he says, "This is for the birds and other four-legged critters to eat."

All the Crooks boys help their dad work the stone. I join right in. Amos roughs out a stone in the shape of a peace pipe. Then he drills it out so it can hold tobacco and be put on a wooden stem. The older boys use files to shape the pipe bowls. The younger boys carve turtles, Bibles, and crosses for the tourists. Clifford uses the brace and bit to hollow out the bowl for an ashtray. Amos has welded a crescent-shaped steel piece onto the end of a drill shank. Amos tells Clifford, "First, you drill a small pilot hole. Then you use that big bit to hollow out the bowl." That isn't easy. Clifford lays the stone on the ground and puts the brace and bit on the stone. Then he puts his chest and all his weight on that brace, and he turns that bit round and round on that stone. An hour later he smiles and shows his dad a perfect ashtray bowl. I ask to try one, but I'm too light and skinny. That drill just slips around on the top of the stone. Doggone it! I'm just happy that I can carve out little pipestone crosses and sell them to a tourist for a nickel. Then I can buy a Hershey bar with almonds.

Those pipe makers know the history of the area. They know about those old-time things, even before the coming of the white man. At the boarding school they teach American history, and our books say Columbus discovered America and the white man went out to settle the West.

Amos Crooks tells his sons and me how his people, the Sioux, had an uprising in southern Minnesota in 1862, and after the Sioux were defeated by the government, they hanged thirty-eight Indian leaders and chiefs.

Another Indian boy from South Dakota tells us about the Battle of Wounded Knee in 1890. His grandma and great-aunt survived the massacre, and even though they were eight- and nine-year-old girls, the soldiers raped them.

I love hearing Indian stories and legends, but this is terrible. I have a tough time going to sleep back in the dormitory. Us Indians were here first, and the white men claim it for themselves. And now, I'm in an Indian boarding school run by the American government. It's the same government some of my friends' families have fought against. When I ask Mr. Balmer about it, he says, "The government has a policy to assimilate young Indians into society." I don't understand what he says, but it doesn't sound good.

‡ ‡ ‡

It's time to go to school again, and my sister Myra looks at my shoes. The soles have big holes in them, and the tops are worn out from dragging on the sidewalks. I broke and tied the shoestrings a bunch of times. My shoes are totally worn out, and we don't have any new shoes in the shoe room in the boys' dormitory.

"Here, try these on." Myra hands me new shiny patent leather shoes that fit me. "Adam, you can have them."

"But they're girls' shoes. I can't wear girls' shoes."

"Adam, they're a lot better than what you've got. You have to wear them!"

The idea of wearing girls' shoes upsets me so much that I get mad and punch Myra right in the face. I can't believe what I've done. We both stand looking at each other. Her eyes fill up with tears and blood drips out of her nose. She doesn't cry; she doesn't yell at me. She just looks at me like she's sorry for me. I feel just awful at what I've done to my older sister, and I vow I'll never hit another girl again, and I mean it. I start crying and I hug my sister.

‡ ‡ ‡

When we first came to school all us little guys were given blue denim coveralls. Now in the fifth grade, we get a two-piece outfit: blue denim pants and a shirt. That sure makes us feel grown up. My brother Curtis says Mr. Balmer told him that all our clothes are made by guys at Stillwater State Prison.

I've been working in the butcher shop for a while. On the wall are drawings of a cow and a pig, with their body parts outlined like a map: every roast, brisket, loin, steak, or chop. When Mr. Brush orders a certain cut of meat, all

I have to do is follow the map. Now I know what the best cuts of meat are. I cut off strips of beef tenderloin and eat it raw. It makes me feel like a young warrior.

‡ ‡ ‡

We just got a bunch of boxes of military surplus clothes and supplies from World War I. I've seen pictures of my father in his uniform. He fought the Germans in that war. Now I can wear a uniform just like my dad.

They give me and a bunch of boys hobnail boots from the boxes. They even have iron horseshoes on the heels. Mr. and Mrs. Burns tell us we'll never wear those shoes out. At night we run as fast as we can and then slide down the concrete sidewalks. Those horseshoes throw sparks everywhere. Yesterday, we tried that in the hallway of the boys' dormitory. All we did was leave deep grooves in the brown linoleum. Mrs. Burns saw the damage and said, "Oh, you boys! You're impossible!"

Now Mr. Burns is ordering all us boys that have hobnail boots to go to the carpentry shop and pull out all the nails and take the horseshoes off the heels. That solved the problem until it rained, and that let water into all the holes. Now all our shoe soles have rotted off.

‡ ‡ ‡

I really like those Sioux and Cheyenne boys with their beautiful noses like the guy on the nickel. I look at myself in the mirror and see a little boy with a round nose. The other boys call it a pug nose. Every day I pull over and over on my round nose to make it longer like the Sioux boys. But it's not working. If it does, I have another body part that is short and could be longer, too.

When we go to town to see the Saturday afternoon matinees, we all get to see the newsreels. They show a new group of Germans called Nazis. They use Indian symbols on their flags and uniforms. One they call a "swastika." Joe Bebeau loves those German uniforms. He goes through our surplus military stuff and picks out a black leather jacket, military pants, and high-top brown boots that he dyes black in the carpentry shop. He changes an American officer's cap to look like a Nazi officer's. Now that he's got all the clothes, he looks

My father, Antoine ("Tony") Nordwall, in his World War I uniform, ca. 1918. Author's collection.

like a pint-sized German officer. He even makes a swagger stick, that he slaps against his boot leg as he walks along. He's knocked out a lens from an old pair of glasses and wears that single lens like he saw a German officer do in a movie.

If you walk toward him when he's wearing that uniform, he raises his arm and says, "Sieg heil!" If you don't salute back he hits you with his swagger stick. It's easier for us to say, "Sieg heil!" than to get whacked with that swagger stick. We all agree Joe Bebeau is our own Nazi. I don't think our superintendent, Mr. Balmer, ever forgave Joe Bebeau when he starting shouting, "Heil Hitler!" when we said the Pledge of Allegiance. Mr. Balmer changed the flag salute to a three-fingered Boy Scout salute, but now we put our right hands over our hearts.

‡ ‡ ‡

I think Delores Two Stars is the most beautiful girl at the boarding school. She's two years older than me. She's got big clear eyes with long, curved eyelashes. Us boys watch Delores change from a skinny girl into a girl with beautiful bumps and curves. Delores is turning into a woman!

Joe Crown, Dopey, or me have never seen a naked woman, and we really want to see Delores Two Stars naked. Just thinking about it makes us boys giggle. We know the girls shower on Saturday afternoon, so in the morning us guys start getting ready to surprise them. We get five-gallon buckets from the dairy farm, fill them with water, and head north of the school to a gopher town in the prairie. We drown out the gophers by pouring water down the holes, and we pick up a couple of buckets full of wet gophers. We're now ready to carry out our plan.

Back at the school we sneak around the power plant to the backside of the girls' dormitory. It's pretty much like the boys' dormitory. The main building has a flight of steps down to a hallway that goes to the lavatory and showers. The hallway has a door to the outside on each side, like a fire escape. We know that one door is near the shower room that is full of laughing, talking girls, and Delores Two Stars—all wet, naked girls! We all sneak up to the door, and Dopey swings it open and the rest of us empty our buckets of angry, wet gophers into the hallway that goes to the showers. We run back behind the power plant, stop, and look around the corner. There we have a good view of the door. The gopher bomb is working, and we start hearing the girls screaming.

"Shut one eye," I whisper to the other boys.

Joe Crown looks up at me and asks, "Why should we shut one eye?"

"My grandpa said if you ever look at a naked woman you are going to go blind. He ought to know, since Grandpa's blind in one eye."

So we all close one eye, and expect to see the door fling open and all of the wet girls rush out to get away from the gophers. Our dreams are crushed when we hear the girls scramble out of the shower room, hopping over the gophers in the hallway and running up the stairway to the safety of the dormitories. The side door crashes open and there's Miss Freeman. She looks like the Wicked Witch of the West. She's screaming at us and is holding a broom like a weapon. She is tall, white, and skinny. It's scary to see Miss Freeman outlined in the doorway and screaming as gophers scramble out to freedom between her legs and all around her. The jig is up! We run around the gymnasium into the basement of the boys' dormitory, and we pretend to be innocent of the excitement at the girls' dormitory.

"That's all right guys. I guess if we live long enough we'll get to see a naked woman," says Dopey Sayers, our new wise guy.

‡ ‡ ‡

The wakeup bell rings at 6:30 in the morning, but all the boys don't jump right out of bed. There always are the sleepyheads trying to get a few more minutes of sleep.

Mr. Burns knows all the boys don't get up, so he walks through every dormitory room with a big Coke bottle full of cold water. When he sees a boy hunkered down in his blankets, he throws a glob of water on the boy's head. That ruins any chances of sleeping in.

We've all seen movies of cowboys and people on wagon trains using long leather bullwhips. Mr. Burns has one of those whips and practices snapping and cracking it all the time. He puts the Coke bottle away, and when he walks down the hallway and we hear that bullwhip popping, we scramble out of bed. Any boy stupid enough to think he can sleep in makes his butt an easy target for that bullwhip. A snap and a pop and an "*Ow-wah-high!*" (Ouch!) starts the new day.

‡ ‡ ‡

Our school library is full of all kinds of books. One entire wall is covered with pull-down maps like window shades. We can see every country in the world on these maps. But the map we like the best is the map of Minnesota. The Sioux boys point out their homes: Morton, Prairie Island, and Shakopee; and the Chippewa boys point out White Earth, Leech Lake, Cass Lake, Ballclub, and the farthest north is my reservation, Red Lake. It goes clear to Canada. My older brother brags that our reservation is farther north than any other place in the United States. And, that map says he's right. And the map shows every road and every railroad in Minnesota.

Now that I'm in the fifth grade I really like to read. In the classrooms they teach us American history about guys like Columbus, Ponce de León, Henry Hudson, Lewis and Clark, and all that stuff they call Manifest Destiny. They say Indians are in the way of progress. I can't understand how all these white guys are given the credit for discovering different parts of our country when Indians were already here for thousands of years. Those stories upset me 'cause I don't think it's fair. Daniel Boone and Kit Carson are American heroes for fighting Indians.

Going into the school library is like going to another planet for me. There are long shelves filled with all kinds of books. The section I like best is the books about Indians. There's a whole bunch of them. We can't check any of them out, so we have to read them right there, even if it takes a whole week to read one book. It took me a long time to read *Red People of the Wooded Country, The Indians in Winter Camp, Little Eagle, Red Feather,* and *Claws of the Thunderbird.* The one I like best is *Happy Hunting Grounds* by Stanley Vestal. I'm reading the book, and I start to cry and I lay my head down on the table. The librarian sees this and doesn't say anything. Little Chief, a Cheyenne boy, was ordered to stay and protect his village while the men warriors went after a Sioux war party. Little Chief spotted an approaching Mandan warrior, and he just laughed at being challenged by a boy in a chief's outfit. Little Chief shot an arrow at the Mandan, but it missed. The Mandan warrior charged and stabbed Little Chief with his lance. Little Chief fell to the ground still holding that lance. A picture shows the skull of Little Chief wearing an eagle-feather warbonnet. I'll never get those pictures or the story out of my mind. I'll never forget that that little boy warrior died defending his people.

‡ ‡ ‡

Sugar Mahto, Dopey Sayers, Joe Crown, and me are looking for something to do. Mrs. Burns says we're "looking to make mischief." We find a big wood barrel in back of the warehouse. Winter's coming on and we know right away what to do with that empty barrel. In no time at all we take that barrel apart. We pick out the best staves and head back to the boys' dormitory. Calvin Iceman is an older boy from Ponemah, and he knows how to bend ash wood into different shapes. Pretty soon those staves are soaking in a big bucket of hot water. Then we bend the ends of the staves over the steam pipes in the basement and tie them down to cook overnight. The next day our staves have nice curved tips, just like skis.

We go to the carpentry shop to shape and sand them. We nail on wood cleats to keep ahold of our shoes. We finish them with a coat of shellac. All we need now is snow. Northwest of the school is the Johnson farm. In the summer the hills behind the barn are full of grain. After the first heavy snowfall it turns into our playground. We never cross Mr. Johnson's yard to get there, because we don't want him to get mad at us. So we walk across the deep snow of the prairie. The bigger boys are in front, breaking a snow trail, and the rest of us follow single-file. We get to the north side of the Johnson farm, and soon the snowy hills are covered with boys. We only have one ski each, and the little guys fall off their ski and roll in the snow laughing all the way. Single ski trails are all over the hillside.

We start our next project in the carpentry shop. We are all following a plan of how to make sleds out of wood, and we're all sawing and hammering. Mr. Sid Garnand, the new shop instructor, is happy to see us kids working so hard making those sleds. We nail heavy tin strips to the runners and paint them with two coats of paint. We even make the rope to pull the sleds. Mr. Garnand has a strange looking jig with small hooks and a turn handle. We tie three strands of twine to those hooks and turn the heck out of the hand crank. We have a three-strand rope in no time. For a bigger, stronger rope, we tie the three-strand ropes to the hooks and crank away on that handle again. Now we have a big, nine-strand rope that we can lift a horse with. We nail that big rope to the sled for a handle, and we're ready for fun. Every car, truck, or tractor that drives past our school on the snowy roads has boys hooking their sleds to their bumpers. Sometimes there's two or three rows of sleds full of laughing boys being dragged along behind.

When Winnewissa Falls freezes it looks like big cliffs of ice. The first drop is over twenty feet down. The lower drops are like giant ice steps that get smaller as they drop off. From there the creek runs under the ice and down to the pond by the rock dam. We start at the six-foot drop, two boys to a sled. We hit the ice with a loud whomp, and then slide to the next drop-off. From there it's clear sailing all the way down to the frozen pond. Wow! That's one heck of a ride! Some of the wood sled runners split apart, but who cares when we can make more sleds?

‡ ‡ ‡

"The Japs have bombed Pearl Harbor! Hey everybody! The Japs have bombed Pearl Harbor!" I hear the radio report about the Japanese attack, and I run down the hallway to the stairs that go to the basement. I shout the news to all the boys like a town crier. Joe Crown says this is the first he's heard about the attack. We've been hearing about how Germany and Japan have attacked everybody around them for the last couple of years, so we're not surprised that they attacked us, too.

Some of us go to the school library to look at the maps. We find the Pacific Ocean, the Hawaiian Islands, and we finally find Pearl Harbor. Dang! That's sure a long way from the boarding school, and we don't feel scared. When we see the newsreels of the awful bombing of Pearl Harbor we figure our country has a big fight on our hands.

Boys sledding behind car. Courtesy Pipestone County Historical Society, Pipestone, Minnesota.

As boys we've played a lot of warrior games, and now's the time for some of us to be real warriors. Clifford Crooks is only thirteen years old, and he announces he's going to join the army. The next morning he takes off for town to the recruiting office to sign up. The recruiting officer takes one look at Clifford and asks, "How old are you?"

"Thirteen."

The officer chuckles and says, "Come back when you're old enough. Then we'll be glad to have you."

Clifford's upset when he gets back to school and tells me he is going to keep on trying. My brother Alton says he can hardly wait until he's seventeen, so he can join the navy. Curtis is one and a half years older than Alton, and tells us that on his next birthday he's going to join the navy. One of the boys asks, "When's your birthday?"

"December 7."

‡ ‡ ‡

It's his last year at Pipestone and my older brother Curtis works for Mr. Balmer. He's his houseboy, and he goes with him to tribal council meetings at Morton, Prairie Island, and Shakopee. Mr. Balmer tells Curtis all kinds of things I never knew, like how he knows we're raiding the little shed at Beede's Bakery in town.

Curtis says that the boarding schools were created to give Indian kids an education so we can be assimilated into society. That's why the school arranges for so many sports and social activities with Pipestone and other towns.

In the summer they let us go to the Pipestone swimming pool and play-grounds, and on weekends we go to listen to the community band at the city hall park. We listen to the band for a while, then we just have to play, rolling around the grass and climbing on the great big cannon that looks like it guards the park. We sit on that cannon barrel like we're riding a horse.

Curtis loves telling me stories about what's going on without us kids knowing about it. He asks, "Did you ever wonder about every Christmas time, how every kid at school gets at least one present, although some of them are orphans?"

I answer, "Yeah, I wonder about that. How come?"

Curtis lowers his voice like he is telling me a deep dark secret. "When the presents start coming from the families on the reservations, the staff has the list of all the students, and when a package comes it's writ-ten down. The shop owners and churches of Pipestone donate enough toys and presents to make sure every boy and girl gets something for Christmas. That's awful nice of those people."

Curtis tells me he has a white girlfriend in town that lives in a small apartment over a dry-cleaning shop called the "Toggary." Is this what they mean by *assimilation*?

Curtis laughs when he tells me Mr. Balmer and Mr. Beede are good bud-dies and they always know when the Indian boys are raiding that little shed that never has a lock on it. He says they stand by the second-story window watching us little guys scrounging around for food. And we think we're really clever and sneaky. All the time Mr. Beede and Mr. Balmer are watching and feeling sorry for the little boys. Mr. Balmer told Curtis he knows we could have more to eat in the dining hall, but something he calls "the federal budget" doesn't allow more. We never do have any fat little Indians at the school.

When the winter snow gets too deep for us to use the parching place we go to the power plant. It runs full blast to keep all the buildings warm, and it makes our hot water. The burned coal and ashes are dumped behind the power plant. That big pile of red-hot slag is just another chance for us to cook outside.

We take syrup from the kitchen and boil it in one-gallon cans over those coals. We cook that syrup down until it's thick and then dump it on the snow to cool off and get hard. We call it taffy.

We get armloads of spuds from the root cellar. Clifford Crooks is a good friend of Harvey Derby, who's a Sioux from Sisseton, South Dakota, and works at the power plant. Clifford puts a load of spuds in the slag heap, and Harvey brings out a wheelbarrow full of red-hot slag and dumps it all over our spuds. We go play for an hour, and when we come back they're done. The skins are burnt, but inside is a steamy hot spud. Clifford always gives Harvey a few spuds to say thank you. We add some salt and pepper. Ouch! Ouch! Ouch! We can't wait for the spuds to cool down before we start chomping on them. Dang, they're good! We share our extra spuds with the boys in the dormitory.

We went to a Saturday matinee in town and saw a movie about an English family who roasted spuds, only they called them "Murphys." Since then we call our roasted spuds Murphys. When we say we're going to fix Murphys everybody knows what we mean.

‡ ‡ ‡

Spring thaw when the ice is breaking up is another chance for us guys to act goofy. We watch huge sheets of ice break off and go crashing over the falls.

We can hop on those ice pieces for a crazy ride. We jump onto the riverbank before our ice raft goes over the falls. Then we run up the creek and catch another ride. That's not dangerous enough, so some boys want to see how close they can get to the falls before they jump off onto the riverbank.

Damn that Sugar Mahto! He rides that ice right to the edge of the falls, and then he jumps to a big boulder under the lip of the falls. If he missed, he would've been killed on the rocks and the falling ice would've ground him into hamburger. Nobody dares to try to outdo Sugar.

The melting snow and ice and heavy spring rains are flooding Pipestone. When the floodwaters go over the riverbanks it makes a huge waterfall over the cliffs above the quarries. That waterfall must be a half a mile long of roaring mist.

A couple of us boys go down and are standing on the railroad bridge watching all kinds of stuff going down and over the falls. We see a small herd of cows standing on what looks like a small island in the middle of the water. One scared cow takes off swimming, but she's caught in the fast water. All we can do is watch. She bellows and tries to get out but the water drags her under the bridge. Her head hits the steel girder and we hear an awful thunk. We run to the other side of the bridge and see her body going over the falls. We walk along the railroad tracks back to school, and all of us are really quiet.

‡ ‡ ‡

After the spring floods settle down, we walk along the banks of the creek looking for logs and timbers that are scattered around. The top rock dam by the pond doesn't have much. There are two more smaller dams at Indian lakes, one at the center, and the other is at the end by the Johnson farm. We get enough logs and wood planks so we can make rafts, and with long poles we float around on those ponds.

"Get off! Get off!" we holler as too many boys jump on the raft and almost sink it. "Go make your own."

A bunch of us boys are on our raft in the middle of the lake acting like Tom Sawyer and Huckleberry Finn. It sure feels good to fish with a willow stick and a string with a common pin bent into the shape of a fishhook. We use an earthworm for bait. It doesn't take us too long before we have a bunch of little perch that we cook at the parching place. Boy, the fish is tender and we feel like life is good.

‡ ‡ ‡

Going to the movies in town is always a special treat. They give every one of us a quarter, and the school bus drops us off at the Orpheum Theater. We run to the popcorn stand that's in a corner of the lobby. Mr. Allen runs the stand, and he's always happy to see us kids and sell us popcorn, candy, and pop. Each thing costs us a nickel. The movie costs us a dime. "Uncle" Charlie runs the theater and shows a lot of cowboy and Indian movies. The Indian kids and white kids all cheer when the bugler sounds "charge" and the soldiers ride to rescue the white settlers fighting off the savage Indians that are circling the burning wagons.

Joe Bebeau gets mad at us for cheering the cavalry. "Hey, you guys, you're cheering for the wrong side."

I think about it and I figure Joe's right, because we've been taught that when Columbus came to America the Indians were already here.

‡‡‡

Our old water tower at the school had to be the ugliest water tower in Pipestone County. I don't think I've seen an uglier one. It was really tall with long, skinny metal legs, a long, skinny tank and a tall, pointy metal top. The whole thing was painted a yucky black. If they painted that black tower all white it would've looked like Miss Freeman, the girls' matron.

When they built our new power plant they tore down that ugly old water tower. The new tower is made out of steel girders and beams. The tank on top is much bigger around than the old one. They put a big steel-ball lid on top of it and the whole thing's painted silver. They built the tallest playground in the world for us boys. Steel ladders go clear up the top to the steel ball. We climb the steel ladder to the top of the tank and slide down the steel struts, zigzagging three times until we reach the ground. Mr. and Mrs. Burns and the other staff have fits when they see us slide down like monkeys. They chase us off, and we sneak back and go up that tower again. Besides, there's a walkway around the water tank and we can see for miles and miles across the prairie. The carnival comes to Pipestone every summer, but their Ferris wheel doesn't come close to how high we can get on the water tower. We have twice the view and it doesn't cost us a dime.

I don't get to go home for the summer again, so I wait until after dark and climb to the very top of the water tower and sit on that big steel ball and I can see the lights of Pipestone a mile and a half away. I'm really sad, but it's so peaceful and quiet up there.

It's the summer of Delores Two Stars (this is an old-time Indian way of keeping a calendar called Winter Count). After we don't get to see Delores

The boys' dormitory—my home for ten years—and the old water tower behind it. Courtesy Pipestone County Historical Society, Pipestone, Minnesota.

Two Stars naked, we keep up our usual summer work details like mowing the school lawns and football field. The girls have to do their work details, too.

I'm twelve and I've learned a lot about how to maintain the boarding school. I know how to glaze windows, paint the dormitories, and now I'm learning how to refinish the floor in the boys' dormitory. We use belt sanders, disk sanders, and scrapers on those hardwood floors to get all that old wax scum off. We put filler in the big gouges, then paint it with shellac, and then two coats of varnish. Those hardwood floors look brand new.

Mr. Caulkins likes what we've done and says our next job is to repaint the apartment above the boarding school kitchen. Mrs. Lucille Blyth, our dining hall matron, lives there with her husband, Frank, and their fat, spoiled little boy who's never nice to us. But that's okay, because none of the kids of the school workers go to school here, they all go into Pipestone.

We refinish their floors, paint their ceilings and walls, and they can move back in a week. Mr. Balmer says this kind of work is expected of us kids, so we can help maintain the boarding school. We don't know or understand why; we just do our jobs.

Ever since I was a little boy, I always go barefoot in the summer at home at

Red Lake and at school at Pipestone. It sure saves a lot of shoe leather. My feet get really tough from running over the rough ground and hot railroad tracks. When we're drowning out gophers at a place we call Gopher Town, northwest of the school grounds, we have to watch out for the little cactus plants that grow around the rocks. When we step on a cactus we yell, "*Ow-wah-high!*" We have to sit right down on a rock and pull the thorns out of our feet. After that we go on our way and pretend nothing happened.

Mr. Burns calls me "tough feet" and says I can walk barefoot over broken glass. "*Ah waah!*" I say, and I tell him about the time I jumped over a bench in the front yard of the boys' dormitory. I landed on a broken Coke bottle and darn near cut my big toe off. The other boys grabbed me and dragged me off to the school hospital, and I left a bloody trail behind me. That doesn't seem like tough feet to me. After the doctor stitched my big toe, me and my big toe figured we ought to stay together. Maybe wearing shoes is a good idea after all. Maybe it means I'm growing up.

‡ ‡ ‡

The war sure makes everybody extra busy. At school we even have to plant bigger gardens. Now we call them "Victory Gardens."[12] Everything's so patriotic, I think they're going to make us grow red, white, and blue tomatoes next. We weed the gardens and pick off the potato bugs.

We have such a big bumper crop of food that Mr. Balmer is cutting the vacations short for a lot of the workers so they can help with the harvest and canning. It's really something to see the teachers, like Miss Riddle, out in the vegetable gardens pulling up beets so the girls can pickle them.

During summer vacation there's only about half the kids in school compared to when school starts. We milk the cows just the same, only now we have extra cream and tubs of butter that we take to town along with our extra tubs of lard.

In the early summer afternoon the girls get a treat—a hike to the national monument a half-mile away. Miss Bedard leads the line of twenty-five girls through the grassy paths toward the monument. The last in line is Mary. Mary was born with a dislocated hip that never got fixed. So she walks with

Fifth-grade teacher Miss Riddle and the girls pull beets. Courtesy Pipestone County Historical Society, Pipestone, Minnesota.

a limp and drags her right foot a little bit. We nicknamed her Slew Foot Mary. She is a nice, good-looking girl, and she acts like she doesn't have a bad leg and like our nickname doesn't bother her.

The boys see an opportunity to be around the girls, and I start walking beside Mary. I'm really shy of girls and I can't talk to them. I try to talk to Mary, but I'm scared. The girls stop to look at Winnewissa Falls, which are sacred to some tribes. The long line of girls starts to snake down the path to the rock dam a quarter-mile downstream. The dam's made a beautiful pond with lily pads and cattails along its banks. The mud turtles lay on the big rocks warming up in the afternoon sun. "I'm getting tired. Can we sit down and rest for a while?" says Mary. She looks tired. We are almost swallowed up by the tall buffalo grass when we sit down near the bank of the pond. The chokecherry bushes hide us from anybody walking on the path. As we try to talk Mary moves around. First she sits on the grass, then she lays back propped up on her elbows, and then she lays flat on her back. This doesn't bother me until Mary starts squirming and wiggling like she's got ants in her pants. Now I'm upset about what's happening to Mary. When she starts moaning and groaning, I get scared. I think Mary's having some kind of fit. Maybe it's something to do with her leg. I jump up and grab Mary's hands and lift her off the grass. We take a shortcut and catch up to the rest of the girls. I drop off Mary, who has a mad look on her face.

Joe Bebeau is sitting on a big rock watching the line of girls hiking by. "What's going on, Adam?"

I tell him what happened back by the pond with Mary, and Joe starts laughing out loud. "Mary was bulling. Cows in heat want a bull to mate with. And she wanted you to bone her."

"I thought she was having some kind of a fit," I reply.

Joe laughs even louder. "You know in the shower room, when your older brother Curtis is jumping up and down his balls are flopping. Do yours flop when you jump up and down?"

"No."

"Well, that proves you aren't a man yet. Mary found out the hard way. When your balls flop up and down and you get hair around your bone, you'll be ready for the next time."

Now I understand. Mary will probably never speak to me again.

‡ ‡ ‡

We get to go to the quarries, and we pick up pipestone rocks the pipe makers can't use. It's fun carving all kinds of things, like buffalos, hearts, turtles, and bears. We sit on the rock dam by the quarries or use the sidewalks at the school to rub and rub to make that stone smooth. Pipestone dust is on everything we rub that stone on. Our pocketknives are real good but slow, and steel files are much better. Mr. Garnand's got all kinds of files locked up in the cabinets in his office, and he won't let any of us take anything out of his shop. Every door on every cabinet or cage has a big padlock on it. Every door in every building at the boarding school's got a big padlock on it. There's no way to break these big padlocks. Every padlock is locked to a hinge, hasp, and pin. We can file off the bottom of a hinge pin with a three-cornered file. When we push out the pin, we can open any door at the school. We rub dirt on the file marks so nobody knows what we've done. We take a few things at a time, and Mr. Caulkins doesn't even know we lost some files. It's a whole lot easier to carve that pipestone with tools.

Now we know how to get into the school's warehouse, and the main thing we want is food. There are cartons of canned food and huge smoked hams hang from the ceiling. We only take a five-pound can of corned beef. After we put back the hinge pin, we go back to the root cellar next to the vegetable garden. While two boys with a pocketknife open the can of corned beef, the rest of us are in the garden picking lettuce, radishes, green peppers, and tomatoes. We all sit on the roof of the root cellar and have a picnic of corned beef and vegetables all rolled up in lettuce leaves. We bury the empty can out by the parching place so nobody will know our special picnic ever happened.

‡ ‡ ‡

Most of the older Chippewa boys from Minnesota and Wisconsin know how to hunt, fish, and trap. Between the rock dam and Indian lakes is a stretch of brush and tall grass almost a half-mile long that's crisscrossed with rabbit trails. It's a good place to set snares, and we catch lots of rabbits.

At the parching place we make hobo stew, out of cut up rabbit meat, potatoes, carrots, and onions, in one-gallon tin cans that sit right on the hot coals. If we catch two rabbits, we make another can of stew. Some of the older boys really know how to cook over an open fire and show us younger guys how to do things like that. Boy, this is really good food!

‡ ‡ ‡

One day Mr. Burns says to me, "Adam, after you finish your detail, you can go to town and see if you can get a part-time job. It'll be good experience." School's out for the summer, and I think it's a good idea. I get a job unloading boxcars on a railroad siding next to a warehouse. Man! Those boxcars are stuffed with all kinds of boxes and crates. I'm working with a crew of men, and we use hand trucks and freight wagons to unload that stuff and then wheel it into the warehouse.

During a rest break, the boss talks to me and asks questions about what I do at school. When I tell him that I worked in the bakery he says, "Come here. I want to show you something."

He takes me over to a roasting machine. "Do you think you could run this thing?" he asks.

This is easy compared to the machines in the school bakery. Now, I'm in

charge of roasting peanuts, fifty-pound bags at a time. I don't even need a recipe. I set the heat at three hundred degrees and dry roast those nuts for half an
hour. I've never burned a batch!

Late in the summer the crab apples and wild plums are getting ripe. We
don't get many sweets at the boarding school, and the ripe wild fruit is a special treat. I eat a whole lotta wild plums in the grove next to the parching place
on the northwest side of the school.

The next morning I wake up with an awful stomach ache. Lucky for me Mr.
Burns isn't going around rousting out the sleepy heads, so I stay in bed, and
the pain is getting worse. I think I'm tough, but the pain in my gut is really
bad. I stay in bed, and in the middle of the afternoon I know something's really wrong. It's hard for me to bend over, so it takes me a long time to put my
clothes on and walk across the grounds toward the hospital. My brother Alton
and a couple of other boys see me fall on the lawn. They run over and carry
me to the hospital.

"Come to the school. Your son Adam is dying," is the short telegram my
mother receives in Sisseton, South Dakota. Dr. Williams is a contract doctor
from Pipestone, and he doesn't have to show up until eight o'clock tomorrow
morning. I suffer all night long. I've never felt such a long, awful pain before.
My guts are on fire, and I scream out for water. All the night nurse can do is give
me ice cubes to suck on. They say I have acute appendicitis, and early the next
morning it bursts and spreads poison all through my body. I feel myself slip-
ping away to a place where I don't feel any pain. They wheel me into the operating room, and I can see the tray with scalpels and other tools. They put a mask
with ether in it over my nose and mouth to knock me out. It doesn't seem to
matter, 'cause I can hear the doctor and nurses talking. Now I'm floating along,
surrounded by rainbow-colored lights and a strange type of sound, kinda like
music.

They say I was in a coma for four days. My mom came to the school and left her
new family in Sisseton. The first things I know are the tubes going into my body,
the painful shots they keep giving me, and little George Walker, lying in the next
bed. He fell out of a tree onto the back of a bench and busted one of his nuts.

I've been in the hospital for a month and nine days. Tomorrow I'm supposed to get out. A beautiful young nurse's aide comes in my room and asks, "Have you had your BM today?"

"What?"

"I mean have you had your bowel movement today?"

"What's that?"

"Have you taken a crap today?"

"No."

She leaves the room and in a few minutes returns with a tray, loaded with a bedpan, a jar of Vaseline, rubber gloves, and a huge pill.

"You don't expect me to swallow that, do you?" I ask.

"Not this time; just roll over." She puts on the gloves, rubs some Vaseline around my butt hole, pushes in the pill, and holds it there. Just then the door opens, and it's my friend Joe Crown coming to visit me. Joe just stares at me and the beautiful student nurse with her finger sticking in my butt hole.

"What's going on, Adam?" asks Joe.

"The nurse is giving me my medicine."

Joe looks at me, then at the pretty nurse, and then to her hand with her finger up my butt.

"Can I get some, too?"

"Will you please leave the room until we're finished? I'll call you."

The surgery's left me so weak I have to learn to walk again. After I get out of the hospital, I stay pretty much to myself and I'm slowly getting stronger. I don't want any pity, even though everybody's happy to see that I'm still alive. Just to be alone, I climb into the attic of the boys' dormitory and sit in front of the dormer window and look out toward Pipestone. It's quiet and peaceful here, but I hear a little squeaking. I check around, and I find a pigeon nest with two little chicks in it. One of them's dead, but the other one's beak is wide open, squeaking for food. I bury the dead one, and after every meal I bring my new friend, Squeaky, some food.

‡ ‡ ‡

Sometimes after graduation some of the kids don't have any place to go for summer vacation while they wait to go to high school at Flandreau or Haskell. Burdette Shearer and Edsel Esty decide they're going to hang around

Pipestone till school starts. They went down to the monument and decided to go up on the north side of Winnewissa Falls where the red stone cliffs get smaller. The boys found a nice spot where the cliff is only six feet high and it's hidden by trees and bushes. They built a lean-to against the rocks from any kind of stuff they could find. They made a stove out of a twenty-five gallon steel barrel to cook with, and they scrounged up old blankets and boxes from the school and made it real cozy. Us guys who are held over for the summer go up to visit them, and take bread and other food. They're like our heroes, the Robinson Crusoes of the Prairie. They gather food from the farms that're nearby, including the boarding school. They catch chickens and rabbits, and they go to the little shed behind Beede's Bakery and load up on pastries. Those boys are really talented and make things out of pipestone to sell to the tourists.

Mr. Drysdale, the park custodian, looks the other way when the boys offer to be tour guides to make a little money.

It's the end of summer, and Burdette and Edsel are packing their stuff to walk to Flandreau, eighteen miles away, to check in for the fall semester. For the rest of us boys watching them go, it's another lesson in survival.

‡ ‡ ‡

I'm a lot stronger and Squeaky's grown from fuzz to feathers. Joe Crown is on the roof with me the first time Squeaky flies out of his nest. It feels really good to see him circling the boys' dormitory. Squeaky's a free bird now.

‡ ‡ ‡

School's started again, and everybody loves going to the Friday night basketball games and most of the employees come, too. Mr. Burns, our boys' advisor, coaches our football, baseball, and basketball teams. All our teams are good, but Mr. Burns is proudest of our basketball team. The basketball team's really popular. It seems like the gym is packed with people for every home game. A lot of those people travel here from nearby towns.

Our cheerleaders really get the crowd excited with their cheers and all us kids join in our chant: "Big Minneapolis, little St. Paul. Who said the Indians, can't play ball?"

Everybody cheers and laughs. Man, these games are a lot of fun.

My brother Alton and Sugar Mahto are two of the star players. The *Pipestone Star* calls our team the "Mighty Warriors," and they play against high school teams in the area, like Lake Wilson, Ivanhoe, Edgerton, Luverne, Sioux Falls, and Pipestone. You'd think it isn't a fair match for grade school boys to play high school teams. Pipestone High School says they will "heap wallop" the Indians. They must not remember what happened to General Custer at Little Big Horn. Tonight, our Indian boys "heap walloped" the boys of Pipestone: 38 to 14.

When our guys play Lake Wilson, the Indian boys pass the ball around so fast the white boys can hardly get their hands on it. We beat the Lake Wilson team 44 to 10.[13]

This year Coach Burns's basketball team scored a total of 572 points, and the high school teams only scored 92 points. Heap good, eh?

⁝ ⁝ ⁝

The school dances are always special events. Before we start, a couple of us boys throw powdered wax on the floor so the dancers can slide along easily. Mr. Balmer hires a small band, called Al's Aces, from Flandreau. Mrs. Wakeman is a really jolly, fat lady and sits on a chair at the upright piano. She laughs and smiles and she pounds those keys with her chubby fingers. Boy, she sure knows a lot of songs. Al Wakeman plays a bunch of instruments: accordion, saxophone, clarinet, and trumpet. The drummer is the guy we like best. We sit real close so we can watch him better. His drums are really different from our powwow drum. At the powwow there's only one drum and it sits flat, with the pounding head up, and it's held up by sticks. This guy has his big bass drum laying on its side, and he stomps on a pedal that makes the drumstick hit the drum. He has two smaller wood drumsticks that he uses to beat the heck out of three smaller, different-sized drums that are on their own metal stands. He plays rat-a-tat-tat and boom-boom all at the same time. Once in a while he hits the cymbals, and he plays all different kinds of songs, even polkas. What a guy!

When Mr. Balmer hires a band, most of the school staff shows up, and so

The Pipestone Boarding School office staff. *From left:* Bea Ojibway, Ophelia Tillman, Lottie Brown, Rachel Laverdiere, and Burnice Inglebritson. Courtesy Bea Lammers.

do some adults from Pipestone. The polkas are a lot of fun to watch, because everybody hops up and down to the beat. Everybody is smiling or laughing when they dance. If there wasn't music while they're doing that, we'd think they're all crazy. Some of our schoolteachers are single, and they all come to the dances: Miss Carvella, Miss Riddle, Miss Mulroney, and Miss Arrowsmith. Some of the people who work in the administrative office always join the fun. Three of them are Chippewa: Bea Ojibway, Lottie Brown, and Rachel Laverdiere. Bea's really pretty and is friendly to everybody.

When the band plays a waltz, all the couples put their arms around each other and dance real slow and close. But not Miss Riddle, a cute, short, and kinda chunky woman who seems afraid of having her body close to a man like Mr. Brush. She puts her arm around Mr. Brush's shoulder and arches her back, so her hind end hangs out over the dance floor. Her butt looks like she's got two watermelon halves tucked under her dress.

When the group of dancers waltzes by we jab our elbows into each other's ribs. Our mouths open and our eyes bug out when Miss Riddle waltzes by real slow. Her big buns swaying slowly to the music have helped change boys into young men more than any other thing at the boarding school, that along with the hope of seeing Delores Two Stars naked.

‡ ‡ ‡

We have the chance to test our courage as warriors, because we're going to have cowboy and Indian wars with some of the white boys from Pipestone. That's where we use bows and arrows. The arrows don't have points, just blunt ends that won't really hurt anybody. We use slingshots on both sides and we throw rocks at each other. This is all good fun, until a white boy brings a .22 rifle and shoots Joe Crown in the leg. He keeps shooting at us, and all we can do is duck behind big boulders.

Joe Bebeau says, "Adam, let's go."

We crouch down low, and we circle the enemy using rocks and bushes as cover. We sneak up on the gunman from behind. Joe Bebeau lets out a screeching war whoop, and we attack the white boy. Joe counts coup on him with a stick, and I grab the rifle and smash it on the rocks. The white boy is scared to death and starts to cry. If we kill him we can call it self-defense. If we scalp him they can call it murder, so Joe cuts off just a couple of strands of his blonde hair, kinda like scalping. We push the broken rifle into his hands, and tell him to go back to his father and tell him what he has done in shooting one of our boys. All the white boys run back to town. Some of them are still crying.

We all go to the national monument. We didn't lose anybody, and the bloody, bruised boys are laughing because we won the fight. Joe Bebeau has even counted coup on the enemy, so it's a big honor.

A family of tourists pulls up. The lady takes one look at us bloody kids and hollers, "Oh, my God!" She digs around inside her car and patches all us boys up. We're warriors returning to our village, and we're proud of our wounds. As we cross the football field, the girls stare at us and start laughing. Hey, that's not the way to honor warriors. When we get to the school hospital, the nurses take one look at us and they start laughing, too. All our wounds are wrapped with Kotex. We don't know what Kotex are.

‡ ‡ ‡

Girls in laundry. Courtesy Pipestone County Historical Society, Pipestone, Minnesota.

The boys on Saturday laundry duty have to learn how to run the great big washing machines, the spin dryer, and the hot air dryer. We have to wash and dry hundreds of loads of everybody's clothes and sheets. After that the girls take over the clothes. They press the sheets, pillowcases, and towels on a big hot mangle and then they fold and stack them. The girls iron all our clothes. They take the torn clothes to the sewing room in the girls' dormitory and they patch them back together. The matron is sure to keep us busy so we don't have time to goof off or fool around with the girls.

‡ ‡ ‡

We play lots of pranks on each other, but the snowplow, sometimes called a wedgie, is the worst thing we do to each other. Any time a boy bends over to pick up his socks, or even in the classroom when the teacher isn't looking, any boy's fair game for a snowplow. When the victim gets wedged, the first thing you hear is "*Ow-wah-high!*" Even the girls laugh at the icky boys when they see them give wedgies to each other.

We have two brothers from Shakopee that are the whitest boys in school. They're pink Indians. They're real snotty and act like they're better than any of the rest of us. At Christmas they always get more toys than us, and they brag about it and really rub it in and that makes us madder at them. One day they're taking turns sliding down the stair banister. They're whooping and hollering to get attention.

Watching them sliding backwards down that rail is just too much for Joe Thunder. He's a lot younger than me. He puts his hands together like he's praying, and when the next boy comes sliding down the banister butt-first Joe lets him have it right between the cheeks. "Wah! Wah! Wah!" The boy pulls his pants down and blows crap all over the floor.

Mrs. Burns comes charging out of the office and makes us clean up the mess and takes the crying boy to the showers. Cleaning up that crap is like scooping up manure behind the cows in the barn. After we finish mopping the floor Mrs. Burns has us all bend over the reading room table for a good whipping.

Later on, we laugh about what happened. Joe Thunder says, "It was worth getting punished just to give him a wedgie and teach those stuck-up boys a lesson."

‡ ‡ ‡

One of my favorite places to go in town is Roe's Trading Post. Out in front of the store they have two funny-looking Indians carved out of wood. There's a wooden man and a wooden woman standing by the front door. They're painted with bright colors, and everybody likes them because they're so ugly.

The trading post is full of all kinds of Indian things: eagle-feather warbonnets, beaded buckskin outfits, peace pipes, and all kinds of weapons. They've got so many beautiful Indian things to see. There's so much stuff they could set up an old-time Indian village right here in the trading post. I've visited the trading post a couple of times, and I just stand looking and wondering about all these things. Now Mrs. Roe has started telling me about the history and people who made these things.

She tells me the war shirts and dresses are over a hundred years old and were worn before the Indians were rounded up and put on reservations. She points to a group of buffalo skulls and a buffalo robe and says, "During those days there were millions and millions of buffalo, only the government had most of them killed to starve out the Indian." Mrs. Roe's telling me stories I can't find in our history books at school. I'm a very eager student. Some of the older boys at school tell me more stories like that.

Old Charley Morrison is a Chippewa. We call him a "Jack of all trades."

Wow! That guy can do almost anything. He does general maintenance around the school, and even helps the boys on dairy detail. He speaks Chippewa real good and knows a lot of stories and legends. He tells us those stories during work breaks. Everywhere I go—Pipestone, Red Lake, or Ponemah—I hear the storytellers. They tell stories I can't find in books. I love all of it.

‡ ‡ ‡

My brother Alton tells me, "Hey, Adam. I got a strange letter from Mom. You know she went to Flandreau Indian School, and she wants to know if we have any Indians working here at Pipestone. You're kinda nosy about all kinds of things. Maybe you can find out how many there are."

You know, that's something us boys never think about. We just accept people as they are. I look for Joe Crown, because he can remember names real good. Joe and I sit at the reading room table, and a couple of other boys join in the game we call Name the Indians, and we make a list:

> Bill Burns, Southern Cheyenne, Boys' Advisor
> Bea Burns, Peoria, Boys' Matron
> Paul Smith, Chippewa, Assistant Boys' Advisor
> Ophelia Tillman, Oklahoma tribe, Secretary
> Art Bensell, Siletz, School Principal
> Bea Ojibway, Chippewa, Secretary
> Rachel Laverdiere, Turtle Mountain Chippewa, Secretary
> Lottie Brown, Chippewa, Secretary Front Office
> James "Buck" Tibbitts, Chippewa, Power Plant Chief Engineer
> Lucille Blyth, Sioux, Dining Hall Matron
> Marion Blyth, Eastern Cherokee, Chief Clerk
> Harland Bushyhead, Southern Cheyenne from Kansas, Baker and
>   graduate of Haskell
> Harvey Derby, Sioux, Power Plant
> Francis Eastman, Sioux, Mechanic, graduate of Carlisle
> Charley Morrison, Chippewa, Maintenance

When we count up the Indians who work on the farm and in the maintenance shop, garage, power plant, and hospital, there are at least twenty more. We don't count the six or seven guys who work for the Civilian Conservation Corps–Indian Division at our new national monument at the quarries.

I go find Alton and say, "Hey, Alton. You can tell Mom we got a whole bunch of Indians working around here. I think about forty. That should make her happy."

‡ ‡ ‡

Nothing much has changed since the war started. We still have our regular schoolwork and chores. The radio tells us to join the home-front war effort like good Americans. One of the ways we can help is by recycling. All of us boys are used to scrounging around the city dump and other places for things we can use to play with. Now we're scrounging for all kinds of scrap metal, paper, rags, and bottles to give to the war effort. We take all the tin cans from the kitchen and bakery, cut off the tops and bottoms, flatten them, and then throw them in big bins that are hauled to town every two weeks.

In the fall after we finish our regular harvest and threshing, they give a whole bunch of us boys gunnysacks and tell us to go out and harvest the ripe milkweed pods. We need to get them before they split open and the seeds blow all over. Their little cotton fluffs act like parachutes. We don't touch the white sap of the weed because it's sticky and yucky. We all wonder why we're picking these pods.

When I get back, I ask Mr. Caulkins, our shop instructor, "Why are we picking this stuff?"

Mr. Caulkins says, "That fluffy stuff attached to the milkweed seeds is like kapok, and it's used to stuff life preservers and life jackets because it floats."

Wow! We really are helping the war effort.

They brought a huge screw press into the basement of the boys' dormitory, and we fill it with all kinds of paper, cardboard, and newspapers. They're all squeezed together and wired into huge bales, just like hay bales. We used to burn all that trash in our big brick incinerators, but now we save everything for the war effort.

All the people in town are busy helping the war effort, too. A small machine shop next to Sturdevant's Garage is making fuses for bombs. The shop boss doesn't mind when us boys pick up steel shavings shaped like coils off the floor next to the lathes. The coils are a different kind of toy to play with. When we get to the city park we're amazed to see the big old cannon is gone. A guy says, "Maybe it was melted down to make bombs, eh?"

It's hard for me to understand why things we used to throw away are suddenly so important. When we have roast pork the cooks save the grease. We put the pork fat in the bakery ovens and render it down to make lard. The extra lard that the school doesn't use is hauled off to town. I really like baking the pigskins until all the fat is rendered out. What's left is a dried pigskin that we call a "cracklin." Darn, they taste great, especially with a little salt. Yesterday I ate so many that last night my stomach felt so bad I had to go to the lavatory and puke my guts out. Those cracklins got their revenge on me. I didn't think I'd ever stop barfing in the toilet. Today, the smell of the cooking grease is making me want to vomit. I don't want to eat any more of those cracklins for a long time.

I go to Mr. Caulkins and ask him why we're saving all that pig grease. What he tells me doesn't make any sense. He says the grease is used to make nitroglycerin or dynamite—explosives they use to make bombs and artillery shells. I think about it a little, and I ask, "Why don't we take one of those bomb fuses made by Sturdevant's in Pipestone, stick it up a pig's butt, and drop it on Tokyo?"

Mr. Caulkins laughs and says, "I'm sorry Adam. It just isn't that simple."

"Well it works just fine with a firecracker and a bullfrog."

‡ ‡ ‡

On his seventeenth birthday, December 7, 1942, my older brother Curtis, his buddy Calvin Iceman, and eighteen others join the military at Bemidji. They call themselves the "Avengers." Curtis joins the U.S. Navy. The rest of us can hardly wait to grow up so we can be warriors, too. We watch for anything that has anything to do with weapons and the battles in the war. I remember reading in the book *Happy Hunting Grounds*, where Little Chief could hardly wait to be a warrior and was killed by the enemy before he was ready. I guess we'll just have to wait till we're ready.

The war's changing things at Red Lake. A lot of people are leaving to go to work in defense plants. My Auntie Angie and her husband, Bunce, moved to Minneapolis, where Bunce works for Minneapolis-Honeywell making valves for the military. They've been in Minneapolis about three months, and Auntie Angie sends me a letter to tell me that somebody broke into their cabin at Red Lake and stole a bunch of stuff, including that beautiful Winchester rifle I'm supposed to get after I graduate from Pipestone.

This really upsets me, so after dark I climb to the top of the water tower and sit on that big steel ball and look at the lights of Pipestone. Doggone it! Here we are fighting a war, and sneak thieves are stealing from people who have gone to work to protect us! I think about it and realize that the rifle can kill a moose or help me rob a bank, but it can't get me a job. I know enough to know, I don't know enough yet. I climb down that big steel water tower, and I know I have to get a good education to survive. I like to think of myself as a good student with good grades. Ever since I learned how to read, I like it and think it's fun. Now I must get a good education and learn how to use the education I get.

My hard work pays off and I get a letter from Mom. It says, "Addie, your report card looks like a teepee village, straight A's. You keep this up, Addie, and you'll grow up to amount to something."

"Thanks, Mom."

‡ ‡ ‡

Joe Crown, Dopey Sayers and I go to the monument to play like we do all the time. We're used to seeing Indian men doing all kinds of work around there, like building picnic areas, paths, and bridges. But, today everything's quiet. We walk all around the park and wonder what's happened to everybody. We go to the shelter, and Mr. Drysdale's sitting on a chair waiting to meet the visitors that come to the monument.

Dopey asks, "Hey, Mr. Drysdale. What's happened to all the Indian guys who work here?

"They're all gone," he's unhappy when he answers. "The government shut down the whole CCC program to save money, and they're going to use the materials for the war effort. The men can either join the armed forces or go to work in defense plants."

"What happened to all the pipe makers at the quarry?" I ask.

"Same thing. They're either in the army, or they moved to work in the plants."

Curtis Nordwall, new recruit, 1942. Author's collection.

With the war going on the government's rationed almost everything: tires, gasoline, shoes, meat, sugar, even women's stockings. People can't drive faster than thirty-five, so they'll save gas. Visitors have stopped coming to the national monument. Mr. Drysdale has to be real lonesome sitting on that chair in the shelter. Now us boys have the monument for our private playground. It's a lot of fun, but we still have to do our work details.

Now that we are at war everybody's really scared about Nazi spies. At every Saturday matinee we see the newsreels, and a lot of people think Japanese saboteurs will land on the West Coast and make their way inland. It's the worst time for four homesick boys from Shakopee to run away from the school. They get to Highway 14 heading to Minneapolis, and frantic people telephone the police and say, "We saw some Japs trying to hitchhike to Minneapolis!"

They're mistaken for Japanese because the boys are short and brown-skinned. The police and local military guys swarm Highway 14 and put up roadblocks to stop those Japs before they reach New Ulm.

All of a sudden the boys are surrounded and taken prisoners. They don't understand what the big fuss is all about. The authorities realize they captured four runaway Indian boys instead of deadly Japs, and everybody is embarrassed. A police car brings the boys back to the boarding school. Nobody wants to talk about it. I ask Clifford Crooks if he or his brothers ran away. He answers slowly, "Oh, no," and just smiles.

"Well, okay," I reply. The more I think about it, I know those weren't homesick boys, those were Clifford's older brothers trying to get to Shakopee to enlist.

Last week five girls wanted to act like tourists, so they hitched a ride in the back of a pickup truck to Luverne, twenty-four miles south of Pipestone. They were looking in the windows of the department stores, and the local police officer, Harry Schneeckloth, got suspicious and took the girls to sleep in the jail that night. He called Sheriff Roberts, who called Mr. Balmer.[14] Mr. Balmer has the girls brought back to the boarding school. The girls are thirteen to sixteen years old and can't understand what the fuss is all about. One of the girls tells me, "We were just out sightseeing." Miss Freeman, the girls' matron, doesn't have the heart to punish them.

‡ ‡ ‡

Every Indian boy at the school has to have a knife. We have pocketknives, jackknives, hunting knives, and even bayonets that were shipped in with our World War I clothes and canned military surplus foods.

My jackknife has a blade that is more than three inches long. The second blade can do different things, like taking out fishhooks. The serrated blade can scale fish, and at its base is a bottle opener. Having a good knife is like having a workshop in my pocket.

Something we never talk about is boils. Darn. Those things get bigger than pimples and they hurt like heck. When Mr. or Mrs. Burns sees a boy with a boil, he's sent to the school hospital so it can be lanced by the doctor. The boys know I'm good at carving wood and ask me to fix their boils. I heat a needle or common pin over a match to sterilize it. Once the top of the boil is open, I squeeze it and yellow puss oozes out until it starts to bleed. I can't stop there, because I have to keep squeezing until the core, or root, comes out. That is the most painful part, and the boy shouts, "*Ow-wah-high!*" Once that core is out, the boil will go away. That's a real yucky thing to do. One way to find out who your real friends are is when you get a boil on your butt.

The bigger single-blade hunting knife is what we use to practice throwing. We put a little paper target on a wood wall or tree trunk and throw our knives at it. Now some of us can hit the target most of the time. Throwing those bayonets they sent us is harder because of that long, heavy blade. The best way is to throw it underhand, and we've gotten to where we can hit a man-size target twenty feet away almost every time.

You know, with all the fighting we do at school it's always fistfighting. Nobody ever uses a knife to hurt somebody else. We use a jackknife to play a game called mumblety-peg. Two of us sit on the lawn facing each other. We take turns sticking that knife into the ground a lot of different ways: overhand, underhand, backhand, off the tips of our fingers, wrists, elbows, and knees. We use both our right and left hands. The final part is to throw the knife over my left and right shoulders and stick it in the ground behind me.

The winner pounds a wood peg into the ground, and the loser has to dig it out with his teeth. He gets his face all dirty doing that, and we all laugh 'cause he looks so funny.

When we go to the Saturday matinee in Pipestone, we watch a lot of western movies. The Indians are real good with the bows and arrows, but they're real experts at throwing knives. Mr. Caulkins says your knife is a tool, so treat it with respect. I keep my three-blade pocketknife so sharp I can shave the fuzzy hair off my arm with it.

I guess you might say us boys are just natural scroungers. We can find all kinds of good things to sell to the junk dealer in town. Something else that we find that's valuable is bottles—every kind of bottles: pop bottles, milk bottles, beer bottles, whiskey bottles, and wine bottles. They're all worth a penny or two. If we get enough money we can go roller-skating Saturday or Sunday afternoon. We must be cleaning up the whole territory, and we find a lot of bottles at the Playmor Pavilion, about three blocks west of the Three Maidens. On the weekend nights they have dance parties. After bed check, some of us boys sneak down to the pavilion. I don't think they sell alcohol, and most people bring their own bottles. Couples take a break in the dance, come outside, and chugalug on a bottle of booze. They throw empties away outside, and we sneak in and pick them up.

Dopey Sayers doesn't like the bigger boys getting most of the bottles, so he decides to get closer. He crawls into a culvert on the dirt road behind the pavilion. He lies on his back, and he can watch everything going on. He holds his breath when a couple walks toward him in the darkness. He stays really quiet and watches them finish a bottle of beer.

The woman walks over to the culvert, raises her dress, pulls down her panties, and pees all over Dopey's face. Us guys are hiding in the bushes, and we have to hold our hands over our mouths to keep from laughing. There used to be a chief called Rain in the Face. We now have a boy we can call Peed in the Face, but we like Dopey better than that.

Clifford Crooks thinks all this bottle scrounging is a waste of time, so goes to the owner of the pavilion and offers to clean up the place every morning after a dance party for only fifty cents. He sweeps the floors, picks up the trash, and mops and waxes the floors. Clifford's found coins and even dollar bills dropped on the floor. He's making a lot more money than the rest of us without getting pee in the face.

⸭ ⸭ ⸭

At school a lot of us kids lose one or both parents, so we know about death. But none of us really knows what happens after somebody dies.

Rex is a beautiful collie dog and everybody's pet. We all look out for him. He knows how to go to the back door of the kitchen where the girls feed him. He was hanging around the boys' dormitory when he decided to run over to the school building. He didn't see the pickup truck until it was too late. That truck ran right over Rex and tore him up and broke his back.

We're all upset to see Rex dragging his hind legs on the road and howling in pain. One of the big boys runs to the emergency firebox and grabs a red axe. He starts to chop on poor Rex, and Rex just howls louder and louder. Finally the axe hits him on the head and kills him. We put Rex in the back of a pickup and dump him in the ditch by the road that goes to the Johnson farm.

Ted Mahto is older than us and says if you want to know what happens to you after you die, you just go out once in a while and watch what happens to Rex.

Oh, geez! That sounds just awful, but we all want to know.

First we had a bloody dead dog. Then he's covered with blowflies and bloats up. The next time we go to look at him, it's stinky and yucky and maggots are crawling all over him. *"Ish! Ish!"* Now it's the end of summer, and we go to see Rex again. All that's left of him is clumps of matted white and brown hair and a pile of bones. Five of us boys stand there quietly and we're really sad. Finally, we turn and head back to school. Nobody can talk for a long time, but we all learned a lesson.

Now that we've seen what happened to Rex after he was killed, we understand why the grownups don't want to tell us about dying. We saw Rex go from a happy, friendly dog to a pile of hair and bones. Some of us boys are having bad dreams and nightmares now and wake up screaming and crying. The other boys understand, because every one of us has had somebody die in our family and now Rex showed us what happens after death.

I always knew it was my dad's death that sent seven of us Nordwall kids to the boarding school. Nobody would tell me how he died, because I was too young to know. Well, I'm twelve now and maybe somebody will finally tell me what really happened. I'm going to Red Lake for summer vacation. I know I just have to talk with my Auntie Anna Garrigan. She knows more about the reservation and my family than anybody else.

She clasps me by both shoulders and proudly says, "Addie, Addie, it's so nice to see you again. My how you've grown. You're twelve, and just look at your broad shoulders."

Uncle Johnnie is sitting in his easy chair looking on. His feet are propped up on a hassock. I go over and give him a hug.

Auntie Anna brings me a cup of hot coffee, and we sit at the dining room table. She asks me how things are going at school, and I tell her how Viola died when I was in second grade.

Sadly, she says, "She was such a sweet, beautiful little girl. I just wish your mother took better care of her so she wasn't taken away to the boarding school."

I say, "But Auntie, Dad dying made us go there and nobody ever really told me how he died. Dad died when I was five, and I don't remember all that much about him. I remember that he was tall and blonde and sort of thin, but not much more. Just things like that."

"Tony was slender and tall," Aunt Anna says. "And he was handsome. He was very Swedish. He had beautiful blue eyes, and two of your brothers and one of your sisters inherited their eyes from him. Alton has the same bright blue eyes, and when he was little, his hair was so blonde it was almost white. The rest of you have your mother's brown eyes; her's are more Indian. You were blonde, too, but your hair turned dark as you got older.

"Besides your mother, your father had two great loves in his life. One was anything mechanical. He loved to tinker with motors and transmissions, engines, radios, and farm machinery. Anything like that he'd try to fix.

Dad, in his World War I uniform, keeping in shape, ca. 1918. Author's collection.

"The other thing he loved was Christianity. Not ordinary Christianity like the rest of us, but the evangelical, fundamentalist kind. Tony was a real fundamentalist. He thought everything in the Bible was the literal truth, and he thought everybody should believe the same as him or their souls would be damned to rot in hell forever."

"That's another thing," I say. "Why did Mom marry such a stern believer? She likes to go out dancing and drinking and having fun."

Aunt Anna answers, "I guess your dad was always kind of religious. He wasn't always a fundamentalist. He wasn't like that when he married your mom and for a long time after that. What got him into fundamentalism was his troubles with your mom when she left him and you kids. That hit him hard and he went looking for solace in religion."

I tell Aunt Anna that I never knew that Mom had left and I thought his fundamentalism had something to do with his being gassed in World War I and spending all that time in army hospitals and never really getting healthy again.

"No, not really," Aunt Anna says. "Tony turned to hellfire and brimstone Christianity only a year or so before he died. It was all because your mom left and took up with Jack Thompson. That kind of thing drives some people to drink. It drove your dad in the opposite direction; he saw sin everywhere and started fighting it."

Jack Thompson is a Sioux from Sisseton, South Dakota, close to where North and South Dakota and Minnesota meet. Mom told me that his drinking and fighting got him into trouble on his own reservation. That's why he ended up at Red Lake.

"The council was going to tell him to leave because he's a troublemaker, especially when he's drunk," Aunt Anna says. "He's a good-looking man and looks real Indian, not like your dad. And your mother was really taken with him. But, when she left it hurt your father's spirit.

"It wasn't so bad that he turned into such a fundamentalist," Aunt Anna continues. "What was bad was that he got talked into one of those sects that doesn't hold with doctors or medicine. Some missionaries convinced him that a true believer doesn't need doctors, all they need is faith in Jesus. In the end, that's what killed him."

Anna said that Dad was such a fierce believer that he thought up ways to get the Word to everybody else on the reservation, whether they wanted to hear it or not. One time he fixed a windup record player with a big loudspeaker in the window of our cabin, so he could aim loud religious songs and preachings toward Aunt Laide's house and some poor neighbors who didn't have a real house but lived in a tent over by the woods. The sound of Dad's loudspeaker went right through their thin canvas walls. Sometimes it was so loud we could be hear it all the way over inside Aunt Laide's house when we were visiting.

"Yes," says Aunt Anna. "And you kids were real ashamed about it even if you didn't understand what it was all about. Tony had a buddy, Charlie Dawson was his name, who helped your dad set that up and blare that record player. He believed everything in the Bible, like your father.

"Your dad and Charlie Dawson nearly drove everybody crazy with all that noise and all that preaching. And it didn't do any good. It didn't win your mom back from Jack Thompson or get her to change her ways. She liked to have a good time. But your dad had a good heart, and he had a lot of responsibility. He worried about you kids. He worried a lot about what was going to happen to you.

"Your dad and Charlie were so convinced they were right they didn't care what anybody thought. They were sure anybody on the reservation who didn't see the light the way they did was a heathen. They could go to church every Sunday and be Catholic or Episcopalian. It didn't matter to them. Everybody was still heathens in their eyes until they agreed to be saved. And if anybody refused, they were going to go to hell. They told everybody that. And, of course, those pagans at Ponemah were unspeakable as far as your dad was concerned."

Aunt Anna knows the people of Ponemah, across the lake from where we live. She knows them better than all the worst things told about them. But a long time ago, a missionary got lost crossing the frozen lake to reach them and was dead before anybody found him. There's still an old monument to him in front of the Catholic church in Red Lake. But the people of Ponemah have always felt that him dying on the way to visit them was a sign to hold on to their old religion.

I remember that I was warned to "watch out for the Grand Medicine men. They'll make medicine, they'll witch you, and they'll do a lot terrible things to you." For instance, if you run a race against a boy from Ponemah, be careful never to step into his footsteps, or you'll fall over. They have powers! Even in a horse race they can stop or trip a Red Lake horse and make a Ponemah horse win with their powers. As children we were taught to fear the people of Ponemah because of the Grand Medicine Lodge and the Medewiwin ceremony. People say it's a good thing Ponemah isn't any closer, but Aunt Anna says that it's just as well that they're far enough away to protect them from people like my father.

"Did he ever convert anybody?" I ask her.

"Not that I remember," she replies.

I only know that Uncle Ernest came and got my dad, and the next day he died, so Aunt Anna tells me the rest of the story. In 1935 he was fixing some farm machine, and he got a cut on his shin from a jagged piece of metal. It wasn't anything much at first, just a scratch. But he didn't do anything about it, and it started to fester. The gassing he'd suffered in France left his blood anemic, and he couldn't fight off the infection. Every day it got worse. No matter how much it hurt, he refused any suggestion, even from his brother Ernest, to go to the reservation clinic or have any doctor see him at all. He said he didn't need doctors or clinics or medicine. All he needed was his faith in God. That's the only medicine anybody needed to get better.

But instead of his leg getting better with faith and prayer, it got worse and worse. When people finally convinced him that he might die, he gave up and agreed to go to the clinic.

"It was because of you kids," Aunt Anna says. "Your mother went off with Jack Thompson, and your dad was so worried about what would happen to you kids if he died. He was in real bad shape when he came to see me just after your cousin Leroy was born in March of 1935. He told me he'd decided to go to the hospital because he was so worried about you kids. I told him it was about time, that I thought it was a lot of foolishness that he let his leg go so long.

"But that decision was really hard for him. To your dad it meant he was betraying his faith in Jesus. He gave up his belief that Jesus could heal him because he loved you. He had the responsibility to take care of you kids."

I tell Aunt Anna that I never knew that he had had this change of heart, and maybe it was because of the pain, or that he was afraid of dying.

"No," she says. "It was because he loved you kids and was afraid of what would happen to you if he died. His brother Ernest took Tony to the reservation clinic. The people there took one look at his leg and said he'd let it go too long, and that they couldn't fix it and that he had to go as quick as he could to the veterans hospital. I think that it was in Minneapolis."

I tell Aunt Anna that the way I'd heard the story was that my father never made it to the hospital, that he died of gangrene or blood poisoning on the train. Aunt Anna's heard that story too, but she tells me that my dad and Uncle Ernest made it to the emergency room, but by then he was so sick nobody could help him and he died in the hospital.

Of all Mom's sisters, Aunt Anna Lussier Garrigan is the one that I've talked to and learned from the most. She's been my real blood tie to Red Lake and the reservation.

Aunt Anna is one strong woman, strong and beautiful and warm. She's not just smart, she's wise. All her life she's been an incredible reader. And even though she went to work full time when she was sixteen, and kept on working full time for the BIA ever since, she's more literate than some people who graduate from college. She's more concerned with people and their problems, and she's more compassionate.

Aunt Anna's kept a Christmas card I drew for her in second grade, carefully saved in plastic. "You were only seven," she says, "but I keep it because it shows you have talent. It points to the road you're going to travel. I've always known that, someday, you are going to be an artist."

I'd completely forgotten that card. It doesn't have much to do with the Christmas spirit, because what I drew for her was a poor Indian trying to keep warm in deep snow.

Aunt Anna was born at Red Lake in 1911, ten years after my mother. She got married in 1930 when she was nineteen and only three years out of school, and she's been married to the same man, my Uncle John, ever since. Both Anna and Uncle John are half-Chippewa. Her father, Grandfather Lussier, was French. Uncle John's father was Irish. Mom and she came from a big family—my grandmother had thirteen kids. Two of them died, and then she adopted another girl, my Aunt Jane.

Aunt Anna and Uncle John have a big family, too—ten kids in all. One, a little boy named Arnold, died when he was a baby, but the other nine all lived and are making successes of their lives. Aunt Anna herself stayed on the reservation all her life. But her children who live off the reservation have never lost their connection with Red Lake.

Before World War I there wasn't much of a school at Red Lake, so my grandparents sent Anna and her younger brother Jimmy to a little, white day-school with nine grades in one room.

We get to talking about what school was like for her and how different it is from my Indian boarding school.

"Well," she says, "for us, going to school sure wasn't like it is today. We walked two and a half or three miles each way, and we didn't even think that was far.

"That wasn't the problem, anyway. The problem was my brother Jimmy and I are the darkest of the Lussier kids. Your mother is much lighter, and our other brothers and sisters also got lighter skin from the French side of the family—the Lussiers. So they weren't picked on so much.

"But Jimmy and I paid for looking Indian. They called us all kinds of names, 'blacks,' 'niggers,' the usual stuff. But that wasn't all. They really picked on Jimmy. There were some real bullies who used to trip him up and beat him. They were downright mean and vicious. And he would come home crying to Mom and Dad. I was about ten at the time.

"Now, one time Dad said, 'That's it. Time to call a halt!' He used to call me 'Squaw' as a nickname. Dad was the only white man in the world that ever got away with calling me Squaw, because I knew he meant it as a joke, not as something mean. Otherwise, that was a fighting word.

"'Squaw,' said Dad, 'Squaw likes to fight. She's one tough girl. Why doesn't she just knock the heck out of some of those white kids?' So I had permission. One big bully always picked on Jimmy. The next time I saw him beating up Jimmy, I remembered what Dad said. And I beat that kid up. I ran at that boy and just beat him and beat him. I was right on top of him, and I made his nose bleed and I scratched his face. And he was down there crying. He begged me to stop. My, but that felt good!

"Of course I got punished," Aunt Anna said. "But you know, it was worth it. They left us alone after that. It took that to make those bullies see that we're human, too. They never bothered us after that. It was all about being Indian. They never bothered those of us that aren't dark."

One thing you can say about Indian boarding school—you don't get picked on because you're Indian. We're all in the same boat. If anything, it's the mixed ones, the blue eyes, or the short noses like me that get ribbed.

"All those years," she says as she shakes her head. "All those years we walked two and a half or three miles each way, nine months of the year. It didn't hurt us, not after they stopped bothering us. Anyway, the worst wasn't in winter, it was in the spring thaw when everything was wet and muddy. We had slush and mud and ice water up to our knees sometimes.

"But, that's as far as I went, ninth grade. I didn't have a lot of book learning, but I had a lot of life learning.

"I never stopped learning. I started learning things for myself, reading at night in English. But, I never lost my Chippewa. I held on to my language just the same as English, and I still speak it as good as I speak English. I had a baby in a baby hammock and another on the way. And working full time. But I kept on studying. I learned about people and about loving."

She starts to laugh. "*Love, loving.* Those words have different meanings to different people, especially when you go back and forth between Chippewa and English. Then you have to translate them in your head. I remember when I worked with the traditional people over at Ponemah. Some of those women had problems in their marriages. They'd come and tell me they were having problems at home with their husbands. So, I would say, in English, 'Do you love your husband?' They would look at me like I was some dirty old woman, asking a question like that!

"One day, I was carrying this little boy at Ponemah. He was about eight years old. His mother died and the aunt and uncle that he went to live with were really poor. They had too many kids of their own to take care of, too many mouths to feed. I felt so sorry for that little boy. I said to him, 'Mike, I'm coming after you to find you a new home because Aunt Josie can't take care of you anymore. It isn't that she doesn't love you; she loves you all right. She just can't look after you anymore.'

"He said, 'Okay,' and he snuggled up close to me. And he said, 'Anna, you like me, don't you?' Everybody called me Anna, even the kids. I liked it that way. And I said to him, 'What would you say if I told you that I don't just like you, that I love you?' And he said, 'Oh, Anna, I'm too young!'

"Well," Aunt Anna said, "loving or liking, it seems to me people got along a lot better with one another back then than they do now—even if they lived in shacks and were hungry a lot of the time. In the old days who locked their doors here on the reservation? Nobody. No matter how poor people were, you just didn't go in anybody's house and take what wasn't yours."

She went to work the first time in 1927, when she was barely sixteen, as a hospital aide. That was two years before I was even born.

She remembers, "We still lived in our old place back there in the woods, not far from the old powwow grounds. And not far from your folks' cabin and Aunt Laide's house.

"When I went to work over at the hospital by the agency, I took that little path downhill through the woods—and those woods were so dark—across the creek, over the little bridge, and on up the hill on the other side to the agency. In winter it was thirty, forty below, even when the wind wasn't blowing. That was some walk!

"This was all walking country then. Kids still walk from Redby to Red Lake, and that's five miles each way. But that's their choice. In those days there was no other way to Ponemah. It was all dirt track. And, when you set out for Ponemah, you took along food. It was especially bad in winter, and even worse in the spring thaw.

"In those days, when you wanted to go to Ponemah, it was better to wait until the lake froze over good, because then it was only twelve miles across the ice between Red Lake and Ponemah, instead of thirty miles going around the shore. Of course that ice it had its dangers, too. Everybody knew about the German priest, I forget his name, who decided to cross the lake from his mission in Red

Lake to Ponemah on foot. I guess he was hoping to convert those 'pagans' over there. And he got lost and froze to death along the way. That was in the last century, but I remember our mothers were always calling up the ghost of that frozen priest to scare us kids into never trying to make it alone in winter across the lake."

After two years at the public health service hospital, Anna took a job as a telephone operator at the agency. She was eighteen then, and a year later she married John Garrigan. He worked for the BIA, too.

"While I was running the telephone at the agency," Aunt Anna continued, "the people there were so nice and helpful. They taught me all kinds of office skills like bookkeeping and typing.

"I started translating between the white bureau employees, like the doctors and nurses at the hospital and the county welfare people, who didn't know any Chippewa, and the reservation folks who needed help, but couldn't speak English."

Aunt Anna has always liked the people of Ponemah. "I remember they used to scare you kids with all that silly talk about the Ponemah witches and sorcerers and unbelievers," she said. "But, when I worked with the Ponemah people, I really got to love a lot of them. I mean *love* as in *like*." She starts to chuckle.

"People always said, 'Those Ponemah people across the lake are pagans. Watch out for them. They don't believe in God or anything.' Of course, that isn't true at all. They're very religious, except nobody's turned them into Christians.

"They're good people but very hard to get to. They always feel like they're threatened by the Christians. They had those missionaries over there, two women from the Northern Gospel Mission, who went in and tried to teach them the Bible. They wanted them to forget all their Indian beliefs. Well, some did and some didn't. Some took the white women seriously, and some made fun of them and laughed at them."

Aunt Anna says she really respected a really old medicine man, Old Nordy, and liked him because he was wise and followed the old ways. "Old Nordy is dead now," she says. "Listening to that old man talk was really beautiful. I went to this one wake over there, and he was leading it. He started out talking about the time the dead woman was born, and he went on talking about her life, step by step, right up to the time she died. And then he started talking about God and life in that other world, the afterlife, the way the Indian people understand it, and the way Christians do. He recited stories in the Bible so closely with such beautiful language. The thing that amazed me was that he couldn't even read or write and he never went to church. How did he know all that? He was a medicine man and a real traditionalist, and yet at that wake he was following the Bible so close! And now he's gone, and even in Ponemah, there aren't many left with the knowledge of the old ways, the old beliefs.

"I can't understand how they talk about pagans anyway, here or over there in Ponemah," she says. "Why? Because they don't put their dead in the Christian cemetery? I've been to some of their wakes and their funerals, and they're as religious as anything. They treat the dead person with such love and respect. They put sacred colors on the face: red on one side, and blue on the other. And, after the wake, they put them in a shallow grave, right near their old home. They put food at their feet for the journey of their soul to the beyond. And, they build a spirit house over the grave, a long low house, as long as the body. That spirit house has a pitched roof, just like a real house, and there's a hole in the front for gifts and food, and for the relatives to talk to the soul or the spirit. Sometimes the relatives of those people come there and sit by the graves for a while just to keep them company. I guess they tell them how much they're missed."

You still see a lot of those traditional graves over Ponemah way, even along the roads between here and Ponemah.

Aunt Anna says, "There's a little graveyard with traditional spirit houses over here, between Redby and Red Lake, just past the little Presbyterian church and the Christian cemetery. I was there the other day, and some of those graves are pretty new. So, you see there're still some traditionalists around, even on this side of the lake. There's one for a little child. The baby was just a few days old when it died, and the family put his English name on the stone next to his Chippewa name."

I said that reminds me of a story they tell around Red Lake, about an Indian who went over to Ponemah to one of their wakes. This guy liked the bottle, and he got good and drunk at the wake. "By the time the funeral was over,"

I say, "it's dark and he has no ride to get back home to Red Lake. So he sets out on foot, hoping that maybe somebody will pick him up. On the way he gets caught in a thunderstorm. The rain comes pouring down and there's loud thunder and lightning. Then a big wind comes blowing in from the lake hard enough to rip a powwow dancer's teepee right off the tent pegs.

"The Indian tries to find a dry spot someplace under the trees, but he's not too drunk and he remembers that lightning likes to strike trees. Then he sees the little Chippewa cemetery by the road with the spirit houses. He's pretty wobbly on his feet and his clothes are sopping wet, and I guess he forgets to be afraid of the spirits. Anyway, he stumbles through the cemetery, and when he sees a spirit house with the back open he crawls right in and goes to sleep.

"Well, at dawn the next morning he wakes up in his wet clothes and he's cold and stiff all over. His head hurts a lot and he's really hungry. Outside it's foggy and it isn't really light yet. So he decides to stay there for a while until the sun comes up to dry him off.

"He lays there sort of half-asleep, half-awake, and suddenly he hears somebody singing an Indian song. The song comes closer and closer, until it's right outside his spirit house. And, when he peeks out of the little opening in the front he sees two hands come real close holding a plate of food. So, he stays still to see what's going to happen. The visitor has come around to bring food for the spirit of his loved one, and he's singing a song to honor it.

"And then pieces of food start dropping into the spirit house through the little window. By now the Indian inside is good and hungry, and he thinks, 'Heck, nobody's going to know if I take this food and eat it.' He's so grateful for the food that he forgets to be quiet, and when more food comes in, he says, '*Mii gwitch*' (Thank you).

"Well, that Indian who's giving the food hears this voice coming from inside the spirit house and doesn't know what's going on. Nothing like that's ever happened in all the years he's been coming there with food offerings. And now the spirit inside is saying thank you. He gets so scared that he drops the plate and runs.

"That Indian guy from Red Lake figures out that maybe this isn't such a good place for him to sleep. What if the relatives of the dead come back to investigate? So as soon as the visitor runs out of sight, he slides out the back of the spirit house feet first, and runs back to Red Lake as fast as he can."

"Well," Aunt Anna says, "who can blame them? You don't want to mess with the spirits of the dead. That's a typical Red Lake story, and it may or may not be true. But it makes a point. We still have our traditional cemeteries, and even people who speak nothing but English now and who've forgotten almost everything else, they like to think of their loved ones with a roof over their heads in a little house that reminds them of home."

Anna continues, "You were only three or four when your parents split up over that Jack Thompson business. We felt so sorry for you kids, especially you, because you were so little and didn't know what was going on. Some weekends we'd pile our kids and you Nordwall kids in Dennis's old Ford truck—the older ones in the back, and the little ones in the front—and drive over to Clearwater so you could spend some happy time with Angie and their kids and ours.

"One time we ran into a real thunderstorm. I'll never forget your brother Wallace. He was busy the whole time making the sign of the cross, and we were all Episcopalians, not Catholics. After we got there, I said to Angie, 'You know, that Wally, he kept making the sign of the cross because he was so scared.' So we asked him where he'd learned that. He said, 'That's what Grandma's kids do when they're scared of lightning, and they've never been hit yet.'"

‡ ‡ ‡

I decide to go back to school after the Fourth of July Powwow. After boot camp and training Curtis comes to visit us at the school. He decides to tell me about how Dad died. He tells me that the train story is right but the details of how it happened are worse than the way I heard it. I guess Aunt Anna was trying to be kind.

"Dad had to stop working when his leg got so bad," Curtis says. "And that meant he wasn't getting paid. Then the people at the reservation clinic told Uncle Ernest to take him right away to the veterans hospital in Minneapolis. They didn't have enough money to buy tickets. Dad and Uncle Ernest hitched a ride from Red Lake to Bemidji, where they'd hoped to hop a freight train. They didn't have money for food or even for a cheap fleabag hotel near the rail

yards. Minnesota was still really cold that March, and they found an
packing crate and that was their shelter for the night until a freight tra.
along. Dad was so sick Uncle Ernest had to help him up into an empty bo.
car. By that time Dad was burning up and was getting delirious. Halfway to
Minneapolis he died in that boxcar in his brother's arms. He was only forty-
two."

This isn't easy for me to talk about, or even to think about—my father dying
in some smelly boxcar because he was too poor to buy a ticket.

If the people of the Grand Medicine Lodge in Ponemah can really use
their power to change things, but my father believed that a guy who died two
thousand years ago could actually save his life, but didn't, that really makes
me wonder. Before the white man came here the Indians didn't know anything about a guy named Jesus, heaven, purgatory, or hell, and now, thanks to
Christianity, Indians can go to hell just like everybody else. I guess we call that
"assimilation."

Curtis tells me they're going to ship him out to the South Pacific.

‡ ‡ ‡

We're in Mr. Haun's seventh-grade class, and I see Joe Crown put a big garden snake in the teacher's desk drawer. Before Joe came to school one of the
guys who worked here keeled over dead of a heart attack. I never even got to
know his name. Our teacher, Mr. Haun, is a great big guy. Now, if that snake is
going to scare the heck out of him and cause a heart attack, I won't be able to
forgive myself, so I squeal on my friend. Mr. Haun marches poor Joe into the
principal's office. Mr. Bensell, our principal, is a Siletz Indian from Oregon.
When Mr. Haun tells Mr. Bensell what Joe has done, Mr. Bensell grabs a leather
strap and beats the heck out of Joe. It's taken a long time for Joe to speak to me
again because I snitched on him. We have something like a code of honor; we're
not supposed to snitch on our friends.

‡ ‡ ‡

After we killed and ate Ferdinand the bull, we got a new young bull called
Pat. Now he's as big as Zippy, the other bull. Those guys are huge and each has

their own big pen at the back of the barn. They give each bull a fifty-five-gallon steel barrel to play with. Zippy and Pat know how to pick up those big barrels with their noses. Pat can hold the barrel between his horns and run the whole length of the pen with the barrel seven feet off the ground. When they get to the fence, they drop the barrel and make a loud bang against the wall. I've seen newsreels of seals balancing balls on their noses, but I never saw a big bull with a fifty-five-gallon barrel on his nose like that.

Pat's pen's next to the barn, and to keep the horny bulls away from the cows there's a tall electric fence. How come that wire fence can keep out a huge bull? We have to find out. While some of us are feeding Pat fresh hay, Clifford Crooks sneaks under the fence with a piece of bailing wire. He loops one end over the electric wire and touches the other end to Pat's nuts. That sets off some kind of bull bomb and Pat starts bucking around his pen. We all jump away from the fence, and we watch a ton of mad bull bellow so loud it can straighten your hair. We watch that bull tear up everything in his pen. He's so mad that he flattens his fifty-five-gallon steel barrel.

One of the boys hollers, "Hey, Clifford, you want to try that again?"

"Oh no," he says.

Dopey Sayers hollers out, "Hey, Clifford, can we touch that wire to your nuts?"

Now when we visit the bulls, Pat never stands near the electric fence.

‡ ‡ ‡

I get a letter from Curtis and he's in a place called Guadalcanal. He's a boatswain on a PT boat.

‡ ‡ ‡

Mr. Burns comes into the basement where a group of us are playing prisoner's base. He says, "We have some runaway girls, and I want ten boys to help round them up." We're eager to volunteer, because we know that whoever catches a runaway gets a twenty-five-cent reward. We pile into pickup trucks, and on the dirt road on the west side of the school we can see their footprints crossing the road. They are heading for Flandreau, South Dakota, eighteen miles away.

Assistant Principal Mabel Berry and Principal Art Bensell. Courtesy Bea Lammers.

Joe Bebeau looks at the footprints and says, "These prints are really fresh. The girls must be in that cornfield right over there."

We make a long line, and on a signal from Mr. Brush, we all run into the huge cornfield. Every fifty yards or so we stop and listen. Finally, we hear the sounds of bodies running into the cornstalks. We've found the girls. Now we have to catch them. With shouts and screams the boys tackle the girls. The older boys take advantage of the situation, and they try to feel the girls as they wrestle them to the ground. In spite of their screaming it seems as though some of the girls are enjoying their first contact with boys.

‡ ‡ ‡

In late August the huge corn-picking machines go up and down the rows and pluck off big, thick ears of corn that're stored in huge screen corncribs near the pigpen. We let those big fields of cornstalks stand and dry out for a month. Pheasants fly in and pick up the loose corn off the ground.

I kill a pheasant with a slingshot and give the beautiful bird to Mrs. Burns to eat for supper. She says, "Thank you. Thank you, Adam. This is so nice of you. So you really like to hunt, do you?" She goes to a closet and brings out a small shotgun. It's a Stevens single-shot .410 gauge. "Tomorrow, after you're done with your work detail, I'll loan you this shotgun and you can see what you can do with it."

Oh boy! I am so excited I can hardly sleep. Tomorrow's going to be the first time I get to use a shotgun. I know how to use BB guns and .22 rifles, and now I get to use a shotgun.

The next day, right after work, I go in our dormitory and knock on Mrs. Burns's door and say, "I'm ready to go hunting now, Mrs. Burns."

She laughs and hands me the shotgun and a handful of shells. She also gives me a leather strap with loops on it to hang on my belt. She says, "If you get any pheasants, you just hang them on that strap. You be careful, now."

I hurry out the back door of the dormitory, past the dairy, past the pigpen, to a big field of corn at the northeast corner of the school grounds.

An hour later I'm back knocking on Mrs. Burns's door in the boys' dormitory with a big smile on my face. I surprise Mrs. Burns and give her two Chinese ring-necked pheasants. The next day I give her three pheasants. She invites me in for supper with her husband, Bill Burns, and little Bea, their granddaughter.

Mrs. Burns is an amazing woman. Her kitchen, dining room, and living room are all one area in her tiny three-room apartment. Back home at Red Lake my mother and all the other Indian women cook over wood-burning stoves. In the boarding school kitchen the stoves are heated with gas, and our huge cooking pots are steam-heated. Mrs. Burns does all her cooking over a small two-burner hotplate. The hotplate sits on a table the boys made in the carpentry shop. The legs are long, and the top is a piece of plywood. The table is so tall Mrs. Burns has to reach up to do her cooking. She keeps her fresh food cold in a small, wood icebox that can only handle a twenty-five-pound block of ice. Every time she opens the icebox door I smell a different kind of smell, kinda cool and musty. Boy! Mrs. Burns is a good cook, and I've never eaten so much pheasant before.

"Buck" Tibbitts, a Chippewa from Ballclub, is the chief engineer at the power plant. He's heard of my hunting skills. His rooms are right next to the hospital. He lives there with his wife and two daughters. Buck brings me inside and shows me a single-shot 12-gauge shotgun with a thirty-six-inch-long barrel. They call it a "Long Tom." I call it a cannon next to Mrs. Burns's little .410 shotgun.

I head out to the cornfields again, this time with a pocketful of shotgun shells and Buck's huge cannon. Now I'm feeding two families pheasants and, once in a while, rabbits. I shoot eighteen pheasants that fall.

Duck season's coming up, and Buck Tibbitts bought a load of lumber and blueprints for a duck hunting boat. Mr. Garnand thinks this'll make a good class project. Soon we're cutting and fitting the hardwood frame and screwing on the waterproof plywood sides and bottom. All the screws are made of brass to keep them from rusting. We put in the hardwood seats and the oarlocks. We caulk all the joints real carefully and then put on a coat of primer paint and two coats of dull-green finish paint. The boat is done before duck season starts. Buck Tibbitts has a perfect duck boat and invites me out on its maiden voyage.

"Yep," he says. "If that boat leaks, you're going down with the ship."

"Wake up, Adam, wake up." Buck Tibbitts is shaking me out of a sound sleep. It's pitch dark and Buck is holding a flashlight. "Wake up," he whispers. "We've got to get going."

I get dressed and ask, "How did you find me?"

"Mrs. Burns told me," he whispers.

Soon we're on our way to Lake Shetek, about thirty miles away. We drink hot coffee out of his thermos. It's cold and windy when we launch the boat—perfect duck hunting weather.

Buck shows me how to set out decoys, and we hunker down in the tall grass along the shore. While Buck is quacking away on his duck call and looking at the sky, I check the bottom of the boat to see if it's leaking. The water is too dang cold to go swimming in November. The bottom of the boat is dry and we don't have to worry about sinking, so now I can join Buck looking at the sky for ducks. Flocks of ducks way off in the distance suddenly turn our way, lured by Buck Tibbitts's quacking.

Pow! Pow! Pow! Our shotguns go to work and we get our limit of ducks. On the way back to the boarding school I'm really proud: the boat didn't leak, we got our limit of ducks, and Buck invited me over to eat supper with him and his family tonight. Roast duck and wild rice have never tasted so good.

‡ ‡ ‡

The tractors are done cutting down all the rows of cornstalks. Now it's time for us big boys to help with the late harvest. The huge Belgian horses are harnessed and hitched to big wagons. All us boys assigned to that work detail pile onto the wagons for a fun ride out to the cornfields. That's where the hard work starts. Some of us tie the cornstalks into sheaves. Some of us throw the sheaves of cornstalks onto the wagons, and other boys are on the wagons and stack them until we get a full load. We get to rest on top of the sheaves on the ride back to the dairy barn and the two silos. By now we're all sweaty and dirty. At the silos we unload the cornstalks onto a conveyor belt that carries them into a chipper, and then the chips blow up a huge pipe that goes clear to the top of the silo and they fly down inside. The tractors and machinery are really loud and we have to yell to hear each other. I look around and I feel really good to see men and boys working together. It sure makes me feel grown up.

Mr. Brush hollers, "Hey, Adam, it's time for you four boys to go in those silos and give the other guys a break."

"Oh, doggone it!" I know what we're in for. We climb up the ladder to the top of the silo. As we climb the ladder down inside, it gets darker and darker. The only light comes in around the blower pipe. The chipped cornstalks and leaves are flying all around us like a green, itchy blizzard. We use pitchforks to spread that silage out and around so it won't pile up in one spot.

After we holler that we're done, Mr. Brush yells, "Okay boys, it's time to get another load of corn." We climb out of the silo and get on the wagon for a ride back to the field.

This goes on all day until suppertime. We take a shower and get clean clothes before lineup in the basement. Then it's off to supper.

‡ ‡ ‡

Now that harvest time's over, it's time for us guys to treat ourselves after all that hard work. After Saturday breakfast some of us head out to the pigpen, where we get a bunch of dry ears of corn from the corncrib. We head across the north side of the grounds to the parching place next to our vegetable garden.

Mrs. Burns's granddaughter, Little Bea, said that Mr. Burns, a Southern Cheyenne from Oklahoma, told the other employees to stay away from the parching place because it's the boys' sacred area. That may be why we never see any grownups around there. I'm really proud that grownups respect our traditional ways.

Some boys shuck the corn and some are out getting firewood. A couple of us go to the train siding where the coal cars sit. Between the big steel wheels are the hot boxes full of oily rags they use to grease their wheels. Boy, those rags make our fires start fast.

We put a whole gallon of shucked corn into a big old cooking pan from the kitchen. We have iron pipes wired to the stubby handles of the pan, so two boys at a time can shake it back and forth real slow and get the corn to turn golden brown.

A couple of us sneak to the dining hall and kitchen to get butter, lard, and salt to put on the corn. We know that the great smell of parching corn drifts across the grounds, and makes everybody else want some. So we parch two extra gallons of corn for a giveaway.

We stop off at the kitchen and give the girls a gallon of the parched corn while it's still hot. They love it. When we get to the gym, boys run over and they start to yell, "Gimme some! Gimme some!" We hand out the parched corn left and right. Even at the administration office, employees like Bea Ojibway ask, "May we have some?"

One of the older boys says, "We have to carry on our old ways." I'm beginning to understand.

‡ ‡ ‡

The kitchen has a big service porch where the girls clean and cut up the vegetables for the fall canning season. Billy Bowstring is hanging around the porch, mooching and making a little snot of himself by teasing the girls.

The head cook, Mrs. Irene Remstead, gets real upset with Billy and chases him out of the kitchen. Billy runs down the driveway, and he turns and sticks his tongue out at Mrs. Remstead. She gets so mad she throws a butcher knife at him. That knife sticks in Billy's back and he falls to the ground and his face hits the gravel driveway. The girls pull the knife out of his back, and he's carried off to the school hospital and they stitch him up. Billy never makes any more trouble at the kitchen. The other boys call him "Chicken."

‡ ‡ ‡

Curtis writes and tells me that his boat was sunk by the Japanese in a battle in the Solomon Islands on August 2, 1943. PT 109, skippered by John Kennedy, was in the berth next to Curtis and was sunk, too. A Japanese destroyer cut PT 109 in half. Kennedy lost one man. Curtis lost eight of his twelve men.

‡ ‡ ‡

Our assistant boys' advisor, Paul Smith, has joined the army. With all his experience of giving orders to us guys, the army's made him a sergeant, and that seems right to me. Only now he can't use a broom to knock guys in the butt to keep them in control. So now we have a new assistant boys' advisor. It's my older brother Wallace, the same guy Mr. Balmer ran over a couple of years ago.

Both Paul Smith and Wally graduated from the boarding school, so they know the way things are done. Only Wally is a lot nicer when he disciplines us boys. Compared to rough Paul Smith, we're glad to have him. Wally's a darn good artist, and I like to sit on the bed in his room and watch him make big colored-pencil drawings of the Petty girls. Petty's an artist that draws long-legged pinup girls for calendars, and pilots have started painting them on our B-17 and B-24 bombers.

Now, with the war going on the best work detail for me is cleaning the administration office, because that's where I find out about everything that is going on, not only at school, but other places too. I had no idea how busy our superintendent Mr. Balmer is. The boarding school is the agency for the Lower Sioux Tribes of Minnesota, so Mr. Balmer is their superintendent, too. In spite of his heavy workload and all his responsibilities, he always seems to be really happy.

In the administration office I empty the trashcans, dust off the desks, and sweep the floor. That is real easy work, but what's tough is when the secretaries try to teach me how to type on the Underwood typewriter. Three of the five secretaries are Chippewa: Bea Ojibway, Rachel Laverdiere, and Lottie Brown. Every so often, Mr. Balmer invites me into his office and tells me stories, including the history of the boarding school. I love all of it. I also like to read some of their reports. Some of them are hard to understand, and it seems like they keep a record of everything. Bea Ojibway says they have to file quarterly reports on all the students in the school. I've gotten to see the records of all the school-age children of the Sioux tribes of southern Minnesota. I also found out why we have to work so hard.

After I clean the office and empty all the trashcans I try to use the typewriter. I'm surprised when Bea Ojibway and Rachel Laverdiere come over to me and look like they're ready to cry. They show me a *Pipestone Star* newspaper article that says that "Four United States Senators [are] recommending

Assistant Boys' Advisor Paul Smith in uniform. Author's collection.

sweeping changes in the method of handling the education and care of the Indians. They plan to 'Eliminate all Indian boarding schools. . . . Transfer all Indian hospitals to the Public Health Service.'"[15]

Bea says, "If they do that we'll all be out of a job, and what'll happen to all you kids?" She's really upset and I'm getting mad.

This is September 1943, and I have three older brothers in the armed forces and another one who can hardly wait to join. There are seven Crooks boys from Shakopee; five of them have already enlisted and two more are ready to go. We have thousands of Indian men and women in the military defending our country from Germany and Japan, and, at the same time, our own government is trying to take away some of our old treaty rights. I may be only thirteen years old, but I love reading about history. I know the government is playing a game of mumblety-peg with Indians. After all our history, I just know the Indians are going to end up chewing dirt.

⁑ ⁑ ⁑

Mr. Caulkins likes to smoke Wings cigarettes, and there's a picture of an airplane in each package—airplanes from all over the world. He tacks the pictures on a large cabinet door in the carpentry shop, and us guys learn every airplane used by the Americans, Germans, and Japanese.

Mr. Garnand, our woodshop instructor, has blueprints and a letter from the government. They want us to make models to scale of every airplane in the war. Our guys will use them to learn how to identify the different kinds of planes—friend or foe.

We lay out the templates on the drafting boards, and the shop hums with us guys cutting and carving those airplanes. I start off by making a model of the P-40 fighter plane that General Clair Chenault and his Flying Tigers used in China. Mr. Garnand is really proud of that plane, and I'm working my way up to carving a four-engine navy flying boat called a PBY. We paint all the planes the way the government wants and then stick on the American, German, or Japanese decals. Not all our planes come out right, and we hang the rejects from the shop ceiling with strings. We have our own tiny air force.

We've always made airplanes for ourselves to play with, and so I decide to get fancy. I glue a metal pillbox with a sliding lid to the bottom of a dive-bomber. I fill the pillbox with wood matches that have tail fins like the small incendiary bombs we've seen in newsreels. I nail small hooks on the top of the plane, so it can slide down a string. We nail the string to the wall at the top of the woodshop stairs. Sugar Mahto hooks the plane to the string, and I hold the other end. "Let 'er go," I holler. That little wood airplane starts down that string and its propeller spins. I give the string some slack, and the plane goes into a deep dive. "Pull!" I yell. Sugar pulls the second string that opens the bomb bay door and lets the matchstick bombs fall out and hit the little cardboard village. When I tighten the string, the plane pulls out of the dive for a safe landing at my feet. The other boys cheer and one shouts, "Hey Adam! We should call you 'Inventor.'"

"Nah! I've got enough problems already."

‡ ‡ ‡

Since my brother Wally doesn't like violence and still wants to serve his country, he's joining the U.S. Army Medical Corps and will ship off to North Africa soon. There he'll link up with British forces to fight German General Rommel, the Desert Fox.

Along with Paul Smith and my brother Wally, more and more employees of the boarding school are joining the armed forces. Less than two years after Pearl Harbor, at least sixteen have enlisted and most of them are Indian. Clifford Crooks hitchhiked from Pipestone to the Morton recruiting office, and they let him sign up. The recruits got in three lines, just like at school. Clifford stood in the back row and tried to act invisible when the commanding officer came in.

The commanding officer slowly looked over the lines of recruits. When he spotted Clifford he demanded, "How old are you, Son?"

"Seventeen."

The officer walked up to Clifford and roared in his face, "Now, tell me the truth. How old are you?"

"Fourteen."

"Come back when you're old enough."

Young Wallace Nordwall in uniform. Author's collection.

Clifford's a frustrated warrior when he hitchhikes back to school.

After my brother Wally joined the army, Mr. Balmer hired Beulah Shields, a Chippewa woman, to be the assistant boys' advisor. She's kinda small, not real pretty, but she's really tough. She doesn't take any crap from any of us boys, and when Joe Crown says something she doesn't like she hits him on the head with a steel ring full of keys so hard it cuts his head.

"*Ow-wah-high!*" cries Joe.

"Oh, just go down to the lavatory and wash that blood off!" she says. Now, that's tough.

‡ ‡ ‡

With the war going on it seems like the whole country is on the move, and it's hard to keep track of my own family.

Shortly after Mom moved to Bemidji, her husband, Jack Thompson, traveled all the way up to Newfoundland on the east coast of Canada to build airport hangers for the military. Then he joined the army, and they shipped him to the West Coast. My mother pulled up stakes in Bemidji and moved west and rents a place in Bend, Oregon. Why Bend? I don't know, maybe the rent is cheaper. Sometimes I just don't understand my mother.

Jack Thompson was loading a ship with munitions when it suddenly blew up. Jack's eyes were permanently damaged. After he got a medical discharge from the army, he went to Bend and joined my mother and her four children: my youngest sister, Gwendolyn, my half-brothers George and A. J., and my half-sister, Babe. Jack Thompson is now a frustrated alcoholic warrior who takes out his anger on my mother. Once, in a drunken rage, he beat up my mother when she was eight months pregnant. He was so drunk and mad he kicked her in the stomach and made her abort a stillborn baby boy. Right after that Mom packed up the two little girls and moved to Chiloquin on the Klamath Reservation, where she rents a small house with a backyard surrounded by a tall wooden fence.

‡ ‡ ‡

Pipestone School is out for the summer, and Mom has sent me a bus ticket to Klamath Falls, Oregon. I go to the big maps in the school library and try to find Klamath Falls. Holy smoke! It's on the other side of the country. That's a long way, a whole lot farther than between Pipestone and Red Lake.

The bus trip out West starts off real slow; after all, the wartime speed limit is only thirty-five miles an hour. Once we get to Colorado, the whole country changes as we go into the giant mountains of the West.

Mom and her new Indian friends, the Porters, pick me up at the Greyhound Bus Depot in Klamath Falls. The last twenty-seven miles of the trip to Chiloquin is really beautiful, because most of the road runs alongside Klamath Lake. I'm amazed to see flocks of long-billed white pelicans bobbing along in the gentle waves. They're kinda like our Ivory soap ducks back at the boarding school.

I love exploring new places. My older brother Alton says I'm naturally nosy. Chiloquin is a small town on the Klamath Indian Reservation. Along with the Klamath Indians, there are two Mexican families, lumberjacks, and a bunch of millworkers. All of them are really friendly. Two rivers come together at Chiloquin, the Williamson from the north and the Sprague from the east. On the south side of town is a sawmill with a huge pond chock full of logs that are going to be cut up into lumber to supply the war effort. The screaming sound of the saw blades goes on night and day. At the same time, two large cone-shaped incinerators belch plumes of smoke when they burn the sawdust and scrap wood.

Life on this reservation's wonderful because I can hunt and fish. I've made more friends: Sonny Porter and Jimmy Jackson of the Klamath Tribe. Jimmy Jackson's father is a good hunter, and we've always got deer meat to eat. Jimmy and I catch trout in the Sprague River when we get tired of venison. I catch a fourteen-inch trout off the Williamson River Bridge. Mom is so proud, because that one fish fed the whole family.

‡ ‡ ‡

A forest fire's broken out in the mountains between Chiloquin and Klamath Falls. The rumor quickly spreads that the fire was started by incendiary bombs falling from balloons that were launched from Japan. Now they're launching thousands of those balloons that drift across the Pacific Ocean that cause fires in little towns and forests on the West Coast of the United States.

There aren't many men left on the home front and they're desperate, so they're recruiting Indian boys from the reservation to be firefighters. Sonny, Jimmy, and I sign up as fast as we can. We get into the backs of trucks with the other new recruits and then ride up into the mountains, where we start to dig fire lines and cut fire breaks. It's tough, hot, hard work, but we work together and help each other do whatever we've been told to do. We carry five-gallon canisters of water on our backs to put out spot fires that start when the hot up-draft of the fire carries burning embers high over our heads and drops them behind our line. We can see those burning embers arc across the sky, and we scramble over the rough terrain to put out the spot fire before it can spread. We chop out fire lines with fire axes and hope that we can stop the raging flames. At meal breaks we get military C rations, but Sonny, Jimmy, and I love it. We work as a team and everybody treats us like adults. At night we sleep near a burned area so we can keep warm, because all we were given is a single wool blanket each. Sleeping on the ground is no big deal, because we were all used to it, except for the rattlesnakes that are slithering away to escape the fire. One tries to crawl under my blanket. I grab it by the tail and throw it away, but it lands on another sleeping guy. That sets off a chain reaction of guys hollering, "Rattlesnake! Rattlesnake!" It's tough getting a good night's rest on the fire line.

Tonight is turning out to be a disaster. We're sleeping near a burn, when all of a sudden the direction of the wind changes and blows down a tall burning tree. The tree falls right into the middle of where we're sleeping and sends up a shower of sparks.

Just then our crew boss rushes into the area and screams, "Evacuate! Everybody evacuate! There's a back fire and we're caught between them!" Everybody scrambles to carry what we can down the ridge to the waiting trucks.

"Where's Jimmy Jackson? Have you seen Jimmy?" I holler at guys running down the hill. I search camp and find Jimmy's under the burning tree pinned down by a branch. He's unconscious and his ankle is all broken and bleed-ing. I call for help, but it's drowned out by the roar of the wind and the fire.

The heat's lighting everything on fire, and it looks like the two fires are going to meet on the top of the mountain. I drag Jimmy out from under the branch and get him onto me piggyback. It's hard but I run down the ridge. The huge flames make it so we can see our way. The last truck is waiting for us, and the boys cheer when I stagger into the clearing. Dozens of eager hands help Jimmy onto the bed of the truck. Jimmy's broken ankle and burns are taken care of at the Klamath Falls Hospital. The doctor lances a big burn blister in the palm of my hand to let out the puss.

‡ ‡ ‡

Toward the end of summer, my mother moves us to Klamath Falls, Oregon, where she gets a job driving a taxi. A military hospital is nearby and her business is good. She rents us a two-room shack. The front room is a combination living room, dining room, and kitchen with a wood-burning stove to cook on—kinda like the one we had at home in Red Lake. We don't have a water heater, just cold running water that goes to a little sink. So, just like at Red Lake, she heats her water on the stove. There's barely enough room for Mom, Gwen, and Babe to sleep in the back room, so I'm assigned the little shed on the side of the shack. It has a dirt floor and bare walls. The wood siding is so old that there are open gaps that the wind and rain come in through. At least it has a little window in the back. I look out it and I get a big shock. Just six feet away, on the other side of a barbed wire fence, is a cemetery full of tombstones. When I sleep in my cot I will be only a few feet away from dead people!

Mom looks up at the darkening sky and says, "It looks like we're in for a big storm tonight. You'd better hunker down."

The first things I want to protect from the rain are all the magazines I have scrounged from all over. I have four older brothers and a whole bunch of classmates and relatives in the military. Magazines like *Colliers, Look, Time, Life,* and *The Saturday Evening Post* all have articles about the war. I always search all the pictures of our servicemen hoping to see one of my brothers or friends. I always read up on the news of the war.

A heavy blast of wind announces the arrival of the storm and makes my little shed shake. The gaps in the wood siding let the wind make all kinds of moaning and groaning sounds, and the door rattles on its rusty hinges. The flashes of lightning are quickly followed by mighty booms of thunder. I look out my little back window, and the brilliant lightning flashes cause all the marble headstones to glow. I lay back down on my cot and cover my head with my blanket. Raindrops splatter on the roof. As my cousin Leroy would say, "Holy smokes!" It seems the whole world is dumping on me.

‡ ‡ ‡

Steve is my new friend in Klamath Falls. Hanging on his garage wall is a beautiful store-bought sled with steel runners. It will be months before the snows come. Right above Steve's home is K Mountain. It's a treeless mountain with a big letter *K* made out of rocks painted white. Since it's the end of summer the grass on K Mountain is turning a slippery brown. I get a bright idea and say, "Hey, Steve, let's take your sled and slide down the mountain on the dry grass."

Steve thinks it's a good idea, and we are soon dragging his sled up the great big mountain. Once we get on top of the mountain we have a great view of the entire valley and of Klamath Falls. Steve takes the driver's seat on the sled, and I sit behind him. Riding down the lower frozen slopes of Winnewissa Falls at Pipestone was like riding a wild bucking horse. Now we're riding a racehorse down the smooth, slippery slope of K Mountain. I had no idea that dry grass could be so slippery. Steve and I whoop and holler as we hurl down the mountainside. Our happy hollering turns into screams of fear, as we head for an outcropping of rocks. Those steel sled runners set off a shower of sparks as we hit the rocks. We manage to hold onto the sled as we fly over the rocks. We finally stop the sled by digging our heels into the dirt. I feel a shooting pain in my left hand. Those jagged rocks had carved a wound clear to the bone on my left index finger. The gash goes all the way to the knuckle. It's kinda strange when you can see a part of your own skeleton. It doesn't take long for that gash to fill up with a rush of red blood.

"Oh, no!" Steve yells in fear.

I look up the mountainside, and now it's in flames. The sparks from the sled runners started a fire in the dry grass, and the fire is racing up the mountainside.

Soon the men from the Klamath Falls Fire Department are all over the mountain. They set up fire lines and let the dry grass burn. The screaming sirens of the fire department and the police make poor Steve panic and he cries, "I didn't do it! It was an accident!" over and over.

The police officer looks at the bent steel runners of the sled and then at my left hand that's dripping with blood. He says, "Okay, you boys. I'll let you off with a warning." And then he turns to me and says, "You better take care of that hand, kid."

Mom always has first aid supplies ready, because we kids get cut and bruised a lot. After she puts iodine in the wound, I wrap my index finger with just enough pressure to close that gash. Then I wrap all the fingers of my left hand together with bandage and tape to protect the wound. It took less than two hours for K Mountain to go from a fuzzy brown to burnt black. That big white letter K really stands out now.

‡ ‡ ‡

It's the end of August and my mother has some bad news. She's enrolling me at Chemawa Indian Boarding School in Salem, Oregon. I'm shocked. I tell her, "I want to graduate at Pipestone. I grew up with those kids. They're my friends and I want to graduate with them."

Mom tries to explain, "Pipestone is over two thousand miles away, and I don't have any money for a bus or train ticket."

I ask, "What about the money I made fighting the fire?"

"I spent most of it on food and rent," she says.

"I don't know how we're going to do it, Mom, but I'm going back to Pipestone."

Luckily, I still have some of my fire-fighting money. I have enough to pay for a Greyhound bus ticket, and I'll have five dollars left over for food. That five dollars has to last five days over two thousand miles. Mom packs sandwiches, apples, and oranges in a brown bag for me. We both start crying when we say goodbye at the bus station. I have a suitcase, a box camera, and my notebook that I've been using for my diary. The Greyhound bus heads back east across southern Oregon.

The next morning we stop at a snack bar in Nampa, Idaho. I'm in the back of the bus, so I'm the last one standing in line for the only restroom. Finally, I get my chance. I sit on the porcelain throne but can't hear the bus driver calling out, "All aboard!" The toilet flushing drowns out the sound of the bus starting.

"Hey, Kid, your bus is leaving!" shouts the waiter, as I frantically run out of the store and see my bus pulling away from the curb. I chase that darn bus for five blocks before I give up. I wait ten hours for another bus to come through on its way to Salt Lake City. The only thing left for me in Salt Lake City is my suitcase—my food, my notebook, and my camera are gone.

The next couple of days go off without a problem. We get into Sioux City, Iowa, in the late afternoon. The bus I'm on goes on to Sioux Falls, South Dakota, and I have to wait until ten tomorrow morning to catch another bus to Pipestone. I don't think it'll be a problem for me. I'll just sleep in the bus depot tonight. At five they push me out and lock the depot for the night. They tell me, "Come back at eight in the morning."

I guess I have to wander the streets of Sioux City tonight. I spent the last of my five dollars in Omaha. It's taking a long time to find a place to sleep, so I'm getting a good tour of the town. I'm getting tired, but I still have to find some place to sleep.

I find a big hotel, but I don't have any money for a room. A sign says there's a radio station on the fourth floor, so I go up to see what it's like. Through the plate glass window, I see a band playing music for the live broadcast. When they finish playing, I leave the radio station to go back down and look for somewhere to sleep. The night's getting colder and the wind is picking up. A tall, lit billboard with a wooden deck looks like a possible bed for tonight, so I climb the service ladder and find that the deck is only two feet wide! Darn! If I go to sleep and fall off, the fifty-foot drop could kill me. So, I climb back down and keep searching for a place to sleep. Sure I'm getting scared, but I don't panic because I've been in worse places before.

It's almost midnight when I walk into the police station and tell the sergeant at the desk about my problem. I show him my bus ticket, and he lets me use a jail cell near the front door. The narrow cot has a rubber sheet on it just like

Stink Dormitory, only this room has bars. It's weird to wake up at dawn in a steel cage. Quietly, I get my things and look out at the officer's desk. I hear pots and pans banging in the next room. He's probably fixing coffee. My cell door's been left ajar, and I quietly sneak out of the building.

I finally arrive at Pipestone early that afternoon, and Mrs. Burns stands up and stares at me with her mouth wide open. "Adam, is that really you?" she asks.

Last summer I grew at least three inches taller and gained fifteen pounds of muscle from all the heavy work I did. If Delores Two Stars can grow into a young woman, it's my turn to grow into a young man.

At morning lineup, I take my place in Company C—the big boys. I stand next to Spud Martin. Now I'm as big as he is. Spud must know the years of bullying, punching, shoving, and kicking are going to end. All my friends see a change in me, too. Mr. Burns knows something is going on, because one morning at lineup he gives us the work assignment for the next Saturday morning. "The following boys are to clean the basement rooms: Joe Crown, Spud Martin, Adam Nordwall, and Dopey Sayers."

The usual way for us to sweep the basement is for each of us to sweep a long section of the floor, lengthwise from one end to the other. Grooves in the concrete floor mark off the four areas. At the end we sweep the dirt into piles and use a shovel to throw it into a trash barrel. I'm in one of the middle areas, next to Spud Martin. Like sailors scrubbing the decks, we all move in tandem and sweep the floor as we go. At the end of the basement we start to sweep the dirt into piles. I sweep mine into Spud's pile and figure we'd scoop up the dirt and throw it into the barrel together—teamwork like on the fire line. Spud accuses me of trying to make him more work, and when I try to explain he pushes me backward. I push him back.

"Fight! Fight! Fight!" holler Joe and Dopey.

Boys run down to the basement from all over the dormitory and make a big circle in the middle of the basement. Spud and I square off with one another. We lunge toward each other with bare, bony knuckles and hammer on each other's face and body. Our noses start to bleed and our lips and eyes start to swell, but we keep fighting. The boys cheer us on. I'm not going to give up and neither is Spud. We back off to catch our breath and glare at each other with mad dog looks. We both have friends in the crowd who are cheering us on. We lunge at each other again, almost like we hear a prizefight bell. We go toe-to-toe and our fists are flying. All of a sudden, I step back as Spud charges in. I hit him with a straight jab to the stomach. He drops his guard, and I throw an overhand right that gets him on the jaw and knocks him sprawling.

I think the fight is over. I'm amazed to see Spud slowly get up to his knees and then onto his feet. He charges me again, only this time he swings an uppercut and hits me below the belt on my appendix scar. The awful pain sends shock waves through my body and my legs buckle. I fall to my knees on the concrete floor, and Joe Crown shouts, "You're fighting dirty, Spud. You hit Adam on his scar."

My other friends start to jeer him, too. Now it's my turn to make myself get up on my feet. As I do I'm glaring at Spud. His face is all bloody. I yell a loud war whoop, and charge Spud. I throw my punches as hard and as fast as I can, and I make Spud go backward. He suddenly comes back at me, and I get him in a clinch and won't let go. His ear is next to my mouth, and I ask, "You have enough?"

He struggles a little and then says, "Yeah, a truce?"

"A truce." We get untangled, step back, and shake hands. All the boys cheer. Nobody ever picks on me anymore. I guess you can call this my rite of passage.

‡ ‡ ‡

I pass the annual bug rake test, but Mr. Burns thinks my hair is a little long, so he gives me a nice, short crew cut. Joe Crown checks my head and exclaims, "My gosh, Adam, you've sure got lots of scars." I just laugh, and Joe starts counting and finishes with "nine, ten, eleven. Dang, Adam! You sure have been beat up a lot."

I show Joe the three scars on my left arm and hand and say proudly, "These are my Ponemah scars, and this finger is my Oregon scar." And on it went until I ended at my big toe. "Each scar has its own stories and its own memories. Reciting the history of each scar is just like the old-time Indians painting winter counts on animal hides to record special events."

Joe says he's never thought about it that way.

I say, "Hey, Joe, just to prove it, I can read you like a book."

"*Ah waah!* he cries, because he doesn't believe me.

I start at the top. "This scar on your head is where Beulah Shields conked you with a ring full of keys. Your fingertips have the scars from when the nun smashed your fingers. And the scar on your leg is where you were shot when the white boy brought the .22 to the cowboy and Indian war.

Joe laughs and says, "I think you're right. I never thought of it that way." Then he adds, "Adam, I think you're kinda weird."

‡ ‡ ‡

A group of boys are sitting around the table in the reading room called the "day room." All the guys are curious to hear about my adventures in Oregon. These storytelling times are when we share all kinds of stories. I show them my newest scars like badges of honor. The scar on the top of my left index finger is still a big, ugly red welt.

We go and crowd around a big map of the United States. We point out over a hundred Indian reservations and colonies. Here at the boarding school we have students from at least six tribes, and while I was in Oregon I met people from three more tribes: the Klamath, the Modoc, and the Paiute. When Mrs. Burns walks by, I ask her something that no young one would normally ask of an elder.

"Mrs. Burns," I start. "I've been here at the boarding school nine years. I know you and Mr. Burns are Indians, but you've never said anything about your tribe." I know my mother went to Flandreau Indian Boarding School, but she never told us anything about her life there. She only told us she got an education and talked about her classes in home economics. I wish she had told us more. She was always busy with us kids, and she never had time to sit down and talk to us about it.

Mrs. Burns sits down, and she starts by saying that she was born in Ottawa County in the Oklahoma Territory.

Dopey Sayers pipes up, "Wow! That must make you real old, huh?"

Mrs. Burns just laughs and says, "Not really. Oklahoma didn't become a state until 1907."

From left: (standing) Bobby Burns, Hazel Burns, Bea Burns, and Bill Burns; *(sitting)* Billy Fairbanks and Jerry Benjamin. Courtesy Bea Lammers.

A whole group of boys circle around the huge reading-room table. We're eager to hear Mrs. Burns tell her own story for the first time.

She continues, "I'm the oldest of five children. My father is Indian and my mother is white."

"What tribe is your father?" someone asks.

"He's Peoria. His name is George Skye, and he is the chief of our tribe."

"Oh wow!" exclaims William Daydodge. "Does that make you an Indian princess?"

All the boys and Mrs. Burns start to laugh and giggle.

"Oh no, not at all," she says when she catches her breath. "Royalty is for the Europeans. Indians don't have royalty." She waits till we quit giggling, and then she says, "I went to public school in the beginning, and later my parents entered me and my sister in an Indian boarding school at Wyandotte. Later, we transferred to Haskell Institute at Lawrence, Kansas, where I completed the home economics class. After I graduated I went to work as the boys' matron at the Kickapoo and Pottawatomie Indian

Te Ata reading the Bird Book with nursery children cared for in boarding school hospital, 1935. Courtesy Pipestone County Historical Society, Pipestone, Minnesota.

boarding school at Horton, Kansas. I had always wanted more education, but I liked that job because both my parents worked there."

"Mrs. Burns, how did you meet Mr. Burns?"

"I met this tall, dark, and handsome man in Anadarko, Oklahoma," she laughs at the memory. "He's Southern Cheyenne and the great-grandson of George Bent, who Fort Bent in Colorado is named after. We worked at a couple Indian boarding schools before coming to Pipestone in March 1929. By that time we had two children of our own, Bobby and Hazel.

"Ever since then I've been a housemother with a hundred and fifty boys every year. I know how tough it is on the reservations. And desperate parents want us to take in their children. This school can only provide for three hundred students. When I got here, I was surprised to see the hospital has a nursery for children that are too young for class and have no home. Sometimes we have as many as a dozen babies in there. We keep them, and when they're old enough they're enrolled in school and put into one of the dormitories."

Boys' dance group. Courtesy Pipestone County Historical Society, Pipestone, Minnesota.

Ernest Coursoll says, "Yeah, me and my sister, Rose Emma, were kept in that nursery. You know, they treated us pretty darn good. They even read to us, and we started to learn to read."

I ask, "Mrs. Burns, can you tell us about the little boy you rescued?"

Mrs. Burns is surprised, because she never wanted to talk about it because she didn't want to embarrass the little guy. So we have to urge her and plead with her to tell the story.

"He was born on the White Earth Chippewa Reservation, and not long after that, both his parents died and left him an orphan. He didn't have any family to take care of him, and the state of Minnesota refused to help since he was a reservation Indian. Word was passed on to me about the little boy's terrible situation. I said, "Bring him here. Even though the boys' dormitory is full, we will make room for him."

Mrs. Burns is not only our housemother, she's also a teacher in a way that really makes us think.

She continues, "You know boys, there are three things we need to survive: food, clothing, and lodging. We provide those things for you here at the

Campfire Girls. Courtesy Pipestone County Historical Society, Pipestone, Minnesota.

boarding school. We give you a good education and job training, and we have the responsibility to teach you how to survive in the outside world.

Us older boys at the table understand what Mrs. Burns is telling us, because all of us have gone through tough times in our lives.

Joe Crown says, "If I had my life to live over, I'd still want to come to Pipestone." Most of us agree with Joe.

Then another boy asks, "Hey, Joe, if you come back and have to live your life over, do you want to come back as an Indian?"

"Heck yeah," replies Joe.

Jerry Benjamin quickly pipes up, "I heard the Indian boarding schools are supposed to take away our Indian ways. Is that true Mrs. Burns?"

"At one time that was true," she says. "The first Indian boarding school was at Carlisle, Pennsylvania, and everything that was Indian was forbidden. They tried to make us white. Since then, the times and federal laws have changed. Now nobody is punished for speaking their language here at this school. When we have school assemblies in the auditorium, the boys' dance group or the Campfire Girls entertain us. They're so much fun to watch.

"And, just look at how many former Pipestone students have come back here to work at Pipestone. We're all proud to be Indians here at the school."

‡ ‡ ‡

Joe Bebeau is no different than the rest of us. He's lonesome and homesick. It's the middle of winter, and Joe and his little friend Cry Baby decide to run away from the boarding school. After the Great Northern Railroad drops off our coal cars at the siding, Joe Bebeau and his buddy hop the freight going north. It's freezing cold and the icicles hang all over the outside of the boxcars. The train slows down before they come to the little town of Ivanhoe. When that happens, the runaway Indian boys jump off the slow train and run to the railroad on the other side of the village and catch another train as it's going north. Joe Bebeau is climbing down the icy ladder, and he slips and falls on the tracks. Before he can do anything, the huge steel train wheels roll over and crush his right arm just below the elbow. Oh gosh! This is awful. Joe told me later that he and Cry Baby walked through the snow to a nearby farmhouse. Joe said he twirled his shattered arm round and round, and left three rows of blood in the white snow. They got to a farmhouse and pounded on the door, and a white lady opened the door and saw a bloody boy standing on her porch. She fainted at the awful sight. Her husband heard the commotion and saw his wife laying on the floor and two bloody Indian boys standing on his porch, one with a shredded, bloody arm. The man ran to his telephone and called for help.[16]

Joe Bebeau's arm was cut off at the elbow in the boarding school hospital. We never hear Joe complain. He is the toughest boy I ever met. As the stump of his right arm heals, Joe has to learn to use his left hand. He's getting so good he can do more with one hand than most boys can do with two.

Joe has to do everything with his left hand, and Cry Baby is still a crybaby. It's so bad you can just look at Cry Baby sideways and he starts crying. One day Joe starts punching him on the arms until he cries. This goes on day after day, and Joe has to hit Cry Baby harder and harder to make him cry. Now he's quit crying. He even asks other boys to hit him on the arms and he just laughs. His arms seem to have turned into solid muscle.

‡ ‡ ‡

We see the first spring robin, and we know that the long, cold winter is behind us and everything around us is coming awake. They taught me about the four seasons, and it's always fun to watch the change. Mother Nature is in charge of the seasons, and by the second week of May everything is green again. The birds that flew south for the winter have come back, and all the birds are busy building their nests.

The next morning there's a raging blizzard and the temperature suddenly drops way below freezing. It's hard to believe, because yesterday we had beautiful warm spring weather. Today winter has suddenly come back.

A boy comes running down to the basement all excited and yells, "Hey! The birds are freezing outside. They're just falling off the trees and bushes!"

"Really?"

"Yeah! Come on out and see for yourself."

We all get on our jackets and caps and run out into the storm, and sure enough there are birds laying on the ground. Some are struggling and some are frozen to death. We all get busy and pick up the ones that are alive and put them in our pockets and inside our jackets. Then we run to the dormitory and let them go in the basement. Then off we go to look for more freezing birds. There's a whole bunch of them hanging onto the bushes in front of the school building. We pick those birds off the bushes like we're picking berries.

We're picking up robins, meadowlarks, finches, and little bitty wrens. We've rescued almost two hundred birds, and our basement looks like a giant birdcage with birds fluttering all around.

We bring in bowls of water and other bowls full of all kinds of food they might like. Mrs. Burns gives us some birdseed she feeds her canaries to help out. I think some of the robins are dying of starvation, because they like to eat bugs and worms, not seeds.

‡ ‡ ‡

"Freeze out! Freeze out!" That's a call for us to open all the windows in Dormitory Seven and let in that freezing blizzard. We all strip off our nightgowns and lay naked on top of our beds. It gets colder and colder inside when the snow comes flying through the open windows.

One by one, the freezing boys put on their nightgowns and crawl under their blankets to warm up. The last boy is shivering from the cold. By then it's so cold we think he froze his nuts, but he is the winner of "freeze out."

Going to take a pee at night is kinda hard when you have to walk through two upstairs dormitory rooms, down a long flight of steps, down the main hallway, and down some concrete steps to the landing where the lavatory is. It's way below freezing and nobody wants to take that long, cold walk down to the lavatory. Somebody just opens a window and pees out. A couple of the other boys sneak to the next row of beds, grab a shoe, and fill it with pee. In the morning you can always tell the boys with pee in their shoes, because they holler when they try to put on those squooshy shoes.

‡ ‡ ‡

The storm blows over and the weather outside is warm again, so we open the basement doors and watch the birds fly out into the sunshine. We pick up the little dead birds and bury them.

That storm was so sudden and so cold that we heard a fisherman was out in one of the lakes in his rubber waders. The temperature dropped so fast that the water froze to ice around him and trapped him. He froze to death standing up.

‡ ‡ ‡

Graduation day is May 18 and it's hard to believe my ten years at the boarding school are almost over. I'm the sixth of the Nordwall kids to graduate, after my four older brothers, Stanley, Wallace, Curtis, and Alton, and my sister Myra. With the war still going on, all four of my brothers are serving in the military. Clifford Crooks made it in, along with all six of his brothers.

The number of older guys going into the military has cut down the size of our graduating class to a total of twenty-four: nine boys and fifteen girls. All the big boys lied about their ages and enlisted. When my oldest brother, Stanley, graduated in 1938, there were thirty-one in his class: fifteen boys and sixteen girls.

As Mrs. Fisher plays the processional on the piano, all twenty-four of us graduates climb up on the stage. I look around the auditorium, and I hardly

1945 graduating class. Joe Crown is front row, third from right. I'm fourth from the right in the second row. Author's collection.

hear the invocation by Reverend Northern. The smiling faces of our teachers and staff members show their pride that they got another group of kids off to a good start on life. Then we sing our song, "Goodbye Pipestone," and it's like leaving my family all over again.

The tears in Mrs. Burns's eyes tell us she's going to miss us boys. Mrs. Burns will always be a second mother to me.

At Pipestone, every graduating ninth grade class presents the school pipe to the new ninth graders. This year we picked Mary Messabe to present the peace pipe to Amelia Aspenwall, who represents the eighth graders. It's a strong message for us Indian students to carry on the traditions, culture, and spirituality of our people, so we can pass it on to future generations.

I hope that someday I, too, will be able to pass the peace pipe of understanding and knowledge to future generations. Next fall I'm going to Lawrence, Kansas, to go to Haskell to continue my education.

Life after Pipestone Boarding School

Most of us who graduated from Pipestone had to consider ourselves extremely lucky and fortunate to receive our educations. This is especially true when you consider our childhood backgrounds. Indian children had to endure and overcome great odds to earn diplomas. Not many were to succeed and many were to succumb to the same conditions they had hoped to escape back home: poverty, alcoholism, and crime. The successful ones went on to become meaningful, contributing members of society. Not everyone will agree with my assessment. A member of my own tribe, whose mother attended Pipestone, has a hostile attitude toward life at the school. The daughter, who never attended boarding school, accused me of "whitewashing" my story of life at Pipestone. The debate over the merits of the Indian boarding school system will continue for years.

Gaylord V. Reynolds's master's thesis, "The History of Pipestone Indian School," clearly demonstrates the challenges that we faced in his case study of the student achievement of twenty students from 1925 to 1952. (Please see Appendix 1 for an abbreviated version.) Unfortunately, Reynolds was never able to do a follow-up study to track the lives of those students.

Instead, I will guide you through the lives of my four older brothers and the accomplishments of other classmates after Pipestone. I admit I am biased; however, most of what I write about them is documented. To tell the full story of my brothers' lives would involve writing an entire book for each one. So, for the sake of brevity, I will summarize their military exploits and civilian careers.

As soon as they left Minnesota, we lost track of my four older brothers in the military due to censorship of the mail. In the States we had a slogan, "Loose lips sink ships!" Sometimes it would take months to find out what happened to them. Based on letters to Mom, my audiotaped personal interview with Aunt Anna Lussier Garrigan, other audio interviews, video interviews, secret military documents, and a compelling letter from "Puddin'," the widow of my oldest brother, Stanley, I have compiled a rough outline of my older brothers' actions in World War II.

Sergeant Stanley A. Nordwall was born August 16, 1922. He attended Red Lake School, Pipestone Indian Boarding School, and Haskell Institute. He enlisted in the U.S. Army on November 5, 1942, as part of the 508th Parachute Infantry attached to the 82nd Airborne Division. He made six combat drops behind enemy lines starting with D day, June 6, 1944. On the first day of fighting at Ste. Mere Eglise, his unit was pinned down by enemy gunfire. From an adjoining foxhole, his best friend, Jack Evert, uncle to future women's tennis star Chris Evert, said, "Hey, Stan, you got any cigarettes?" As the two men reached across to hand over the cigarette, a German machine gun opened fire, killing Jack and wounding Stanley in the hand.

In the first forty days of combat, Stanley's unit of 2,055 men suffered 321 killed, 660 wounded (including Stanley), and 458 missing. By July 15, the unit captured 554 Germans, seventy-five vehicles, and eight field artillery pieces 75 mm or larger. And, the 508th destroyed twenty tanks and gained 30 miles by "forward elements of the regiment with no friendly troops to the front."[1] Stanley fought at the Battle of the Bulge, he helped liberate Brussels, and he participated in Operation Market-Garden, the largest airdrop of the war. They took the bridge at Nijmegan over heavy German resistance.

On his sixth and final drop behind enemy lines, Stanley was listed as missing in action for twenty-two days. He'd been captured by the Germans and put into a military concentration camp. He escaped by slitting the throat of a German guard with the folded lid of a tin can. If he'd been recaptured he could have been shot for killing the guard. He eluded the solders and made his way on foot to Allied forces in Belgium. I wonder if those warrior games we played at Pipestone helped Stanley's survival skills in the war.

At least three of the six combat drops Stanley made have been made into movies: *The Longest Day, A Bridge Too Far,* and *The Battle of the Bulge.* He received the Presidential Unit Citation, Bronze Star, Purple Heart, American Theater Service Medal, European African Service Medal, Eastern Theater Service Medal, Bronze Arrow, Orange Lanyard presented by King Baudouin

Colonel McLean awarding citations to Stanley at Ft. Myer, Virginia, 1950. Four different countries awarded Stanley A. Nordwall citations for gallant bravery in World War II: France, Belgium, the Netherlands, and the United States. Author's collection.

of Belgium, and, later, his unit was honored by Queen Juliana of Holland, which was liberated in May 1945. Stanley was reputed to have been the most decorated man in his outfit.

After the war Stanley married Helen (Puddin') and had four children. He started a canvas sail-making shop in Joppatowne, Maryland. One day, after cashing his government retirement check, he was confronted by three young hoodlums who demanded his money. Stanley's reaction was sudden and brutal. He smashed his open palm into the nose of the first thug and splattered blood all over his face. Then he turned and leg-whipped the second thug, and sent him sprawling on his back with a broken leg. The third thug could only swear, turn, and run away to avoid getting hurt. Over dinner that evening, Stanley told his wife and children about the incident. They all laughed and

Wally Nordwall, Mickey Rooney, Bobby Breen, and Stanley Nordwall, Europe, 1945.
Author's collection.

his wife said those punks should know better than to pick a fight with an old
warrior! Stanley died in Florida at the age of seventy-six.

Corporal Wallace Nordwall attended Red Lake School, Pipestone Indian
Boarding School, and Haskell Institute. He enlisted in 1942 as a U.S. Army
medic. We could never fully put together Wally's sketchy war history. He was
the silent one, who refused to tell his first-person account as a medic in front-
line combat. What we know of his military records is that Wally landed in
North Africa in late 1942 with American forces who linked up with the British
and defeated General Erwin Rommel, the Desert Fox, on May 12, 1943. He
then participated in the invasion of Sicily on August 10, 1943, and later its lib-
eration. Then it was on to Anzio Beach, Italy, on September 3, 1943, one of
the longest and bloodiest beach landings. The four-month stalemate result-
ed in the loss of thousands of our young men from the shore batteries and

heavy guns of the Germans. The smells of the dead and dying, along with the screams of the wounded, had to have made an indelible impression on Wally.

When I was the first to arrive at the scene of automobile accidents, on two separate occasions, the young men had their skulls split open. The smell of brains and blood was sickening. The gurgling and rattling of the dying is a sound no one can ever forget. What Wally experienced was over one hundred times worse than my limited experience. He also had to contend with cannon, mortar, and machine gun fire. Wally never got over those bloody, brutal events of history, as he went on to become a very quiet and moody alcoholic. Repeated efforts to check him into veterans hospitals to treat his post-traumatic stress syndrome failed, because he simply walked away. Early one morning I received a phone call from the San Jose, California, Police Department reporting my brother, Wally, was found dead lying next to an abandoned car he called home. He was seventy-three years old when he died.

Lieutenant Commander Curtis C. Nordwall was born on December 7, 1925. If I were to write a book about the wartime exploits of Curtis, I would title it *Ogichida: A Chippewa Warrior in the South Pacific*. A group of young men from Red Lake called themselves "The Avengers," and went to Bemidji to enlist in the armed forces on Curtis's seventeenth birthday in 1942. Curtis joined the U.S. Navy, and immediately after boot camp and follow-up training on PT (patrol torpedo) boats, his unit was shipped off to the South Pacific, where he was a boatswain in a squadron of PT boats. On their first day at Guadalcanal, they were attacked by Japanese bombers, and that became an almost-daily event. In the following months Curtis and his unit tried to destroy Japanese shipping, especially the Japanese barges loaded with soldiers that were sent to reinforce the garrison on the island. Curtis received his first of many medals for coming up with a strategy that effectively sunk the barges with all men aboard. He saw hundreds of Japanese soldiers drown. He could not tell me about it for many years.

During a violent southern Pacific storm, three PT boats broke their moorings with a supply ship, and drifted off into the darkness. Curtis and his crew were ordered to retrieve the boats in the stormy waters. After finding the first boat, Curtis's crew was replaced with a fresh crew who set off to rescue the

Lieutenant Commander Curtis Nordwall. Author's collection.

second boat. Curtis's exhausted crew was called again, and they went out to find the third PT boat, which by now had run aground on a Japanese-held island. Ignoring the hail of enemy bullets, Curtis and his crew towed the wayward PT boat back to the PT tender. For his heroic action, he was given a battlefield promotion.

Curtis told us in detail of the island-hopping battles to regain control of the Pacific. In one secret mission, based on breaking the Japanese code JN25, the PT boats were to line the route of Admiral Yamamoto from Rabaul, New Britain Island, to Bougainville Island, both in the Solomon Sea. Yamamoto was the mastermind behind the sneak attack on Pearl Harbor. P-38 fighters were sent to shoot down Yamamoto's plane. Any wreckage that went into the ocean was to be picked up by the PT boats, as historic events now reveal. Yamamoto's plane crashed on Bougainville; the admiral was dead.

Another code breaking report, JP25, told of an impending invasion of a small Pacific island near Guadalcanal. The only inhabitants were defenseless natives. Curtis and his crew evacuated the island in an all-night effort. At dawn, the Japanese fleet bombarded the now-abandoned island. The grateful natives made Curtis a chief, and the U.S. government awarded him a Silver Star. This is a story Curtis chose to ignore in the video interview with his granddaughter Stacey, for he was too embarrassed to tell the full story. He gave his medal to his girlfriend in Pipestone, Minnesota, who lived in a small apartment above a dry cleaning shop called the Toggary. When they broke up, the girl kept the medal, saying, "If any woman can date Curtis Nordwall, they deserve a medal." Curtis was crushed by her attitude and never requested a replacement for his lost medal.

In the Battle of the Solomon Islands, Curtis's PT boat was berthed next to PT 109. Their skipper was a young, handsome man named John Kennedy. On the night of August 2, 1943, while both boats were on patrol, Jack Kennedy's boat was cut in half by a Japanese destroyer. Curtis's boat was blown out of the water by another destroyer. Most of Kennedy's crew survived after being rescued by natives several days later. Curtis lost eight of his twelve-man crew.

At the epic battle of Leyte Gulf in the Philippines, three squadrons of PT boats were sent to delay the escaping Japanese fleet while our big warships and aircraft carriers moved in for the kill, which would destroy the Japanese fleet's ability to fight any large-scale battles again. Curtis's PT boat was sunk by a five-inch shell from a Japanese destroyer, and as the destroyer passed the wreckage of the boat, the Japanese sailors shot the helpless Americans. Curtis slipped out of his life jacket and used the armhole to breathe through. Only he and one other crewman survived out of his crew of twelve. Two hours later they were picked up by a "buddy" boat. He saw twenty of his crewmates die in two battles.

In a move that was a surprise to the PT boat squadrons, several were ordered to the Aleutian Islands to liberate Kiska and the Attu Islands from the Japanese—the only enemy-held territory in North America. While patrolling the Aleutian Islands, Curtis's PT boat suffered the embarrassment of running out of gas next to an enemy-held island. A Japanese launch took all men aboard prisoner, and just like a scene out of a Hollywood movie, a United States destroyer came around the island and rescued the American crew, taking the Japanese prisoners. Curtis's surprised reaction was, "We were prisoners of war for only ten minutes."

After that, they were ordered back to the South Pacific.

While on patrol north of the Philippines, they spotted a Japanese submarine on the surface recharging its batteries. At full throttle, they ran at the Japanese sub, which went into a crash dive to elude the PT boat. Curtis said they dropped marker buoys over the last sighting, and as they circled, they armed the depth charges and "hedgehog proximity" fuse explosives. "All hell broke loose with the explosions, and soon we saw wreckage, oil, and body parts floating to the surface. We had sunk a Japanese sub!"

"Why didn't you tell me about this before?" I asked Curtis.

His response was cryptic: "You never asked!"

That verbal exchange occurred only two weeks before he died.

With the end of the Japanese conflict, another one was breaking out in China. The communist forces under Mao Tse-tung were overthrowing Chiang Kai-shek of the Nationalist Party, whom the U.S. government backed. In another American covert operation, Curtis, now on a destroyer, evacuated hundreds of American citizens to safety from mainland China. Shortly after that, another conflict broke out when North Korea invaded

South Korea. Before attacking shore installations at Wonsan Harbor, two wooden-hulled minesweepers went to clear the way. Alton was on one of them, the USS *Dexterous*, and, only a few hundred yards behind, Curtis was on a destroyer. The two brothers never knew how close they were until after the war.

On May 21, 1956, Curtis saw the test of the first aerial hydrogen bomb (equivalent to ten million tons of TNT) at Namu Atoll, near Bikini in the Marshall Islands.

Curtis continued his naval career as a submariner and served on the atomic-powered submarine *Skate*. They created history by being the first sub to go under the polar ice cap, linking the Atlantic Ocean to the Pacific Ocean. Later he served as Chief Ballistic Missile Officer on the *Simon Bolivar*, code named SUBRON-14. On a top-secret mission in the North Atlantic, Curtis targeted his boat's atomic warhead missiles on Soviet installations, including the Kremlin itself, during the Cold War.

Curtis retired from the U.S. Navy with the rank of lieutenant commander in 1967. As Curtis looked down on his officer's tunic, he showed me three rows of campaign ribbons, loaded with bronze and silver stars. The bronze star represents a single engagement in combat and the silver star represents five engagements. There were so many combat stars he couldn't explain them all. As for his chest full of eight medals, he seemed proudest of his good conduct medal.

After serving his country for twenty-five years, Curtis turned his attention to serving the Indian people. He went to work for the Bureau of Indian Affairs as superintendent for the Havasupai and Walapai tribes at Peach Springs, Arizona. Then he transferred to Sells, Arizona, and served as superintendent for the Papago Tribe until his retirement. He died at age seventy-six.

Seaman First Class Alton Nordwall joined the U.S. Navy on his seventeenth birthday, June 5, 1944. He went to school at St. Mary's Catholic School, Pipestone Indian Boarding School, Haskell Institute, and Kansas University. He finished boot camp and was shipped out to the South Pacific. But by that time the war in the Pacific was winding down, so he missed combat in the Pacific Theater. We never knew where he went at that time and he never told us. We picked up his trail when the Korean War broke out. He had been

Alton Nordwall, Seaman First Class, served in World War II and Korea. Author's collection.

assigned to a wooden-hulled minesweeper, the USS *Dexterous*. They were to clear Wonsan Harbor before a planned Allied invasion. The constant danger of setting off a mine at close quarters or of being hit by enemy shore batteries kept the entire crew on edge. On one occasion they pulled up alongside a huge mine that was as big as a Volkswagen. Alton reached over the ship railing and touched that monster. One of his buddies called out a warning, "What if it blows up?"

Alton calmly replied, "We'd never know, now, would we?"

After clearing the mines out of Wonsan Harbor, Alton and his crew were followed by a fleet of U.S. destroyers, who then battered the Korean shore installations. On one of those destroyers was our other brother, Curtis. Alton received a pass for shore leave, and he was dropped off in Tokyo. The *Dexterous* sailed back to Korea and two days later it was hit by shore fire, killing six of Alton's crewmates. That little minesweeper received five battle stars.

Alton never lost his taste for education. He returned to Haskell Indian Institute and completed two years in post-graduate courses in the commercial department. He went on to attend Kansas University under the GI Bill. He married his boarding school sweetheart, Eva Fields, of Pawnee and Cherokee heritage, and they had four children. Alton went to work for the BIA in Muskogee, Oklahoma, and in a few years he was the area director for the Bureau of Indian Affairs. He passed away at age seventy-seven.

A fitting tribute to my older brothers' contribution during World War II is contained in the certificate shown on the following page.

Other graduates of my generation at Pipestone went on to carve out careers of their own. At least three boys I knew became tribal chairmen. Percy Powless, an Oneida from Wisconsin, told me, "I never had any difficulty finding a job. The boarding school taught me so many job skills, it was easy for me to find work." Percy returned to Green Bay, Wisconsin, and was elected tribal chairman. His tribe had lost over three-fourths of their land because of the Dawes Act. Percy opened a financially successful bingo hall on the reservation, and after the passage of the 1988 Indian Gaming Act, it grew into the largest, most lucrative Indian casino in Wisconsin. He literally transformed the reservation with the revenue generated from the casino and constructed

The flag of the United States of America flew over the U.S. Capitol on March 23, 1998, in honor of Stanley, Wallace, Curtis, and Alton Nordwall. Author's collection.

an educational center, tribal museum, law center, senior center, and other tribal enterprises.

All seven Crooks brothers from Shakopee served in World War II. Like the Oneidas, they were distressed to find their Mdewakanton Sioux reservation shrunk to a dangerously small size (only 1,250 acres) because of white encroachment in what was turning out to be an upscale suburb of Minneapolis/St. Paul. Norman Crooks (Amos's brother) was elected tribal chairman. Norman and Amos opened a bingo parlor on the shore of Prior Lake called "Little Six," after a famous Mdewakanton chief who was hung for alleged crimes against the government. The Little Six casino spawned the development of the hugely successful Mystic Lakes Casino, to date the largest in Minnesota. The revenue generated provides beautiful homes for the formerly impoverished members of the tribe. It also pays for tribal health care, education, and generous per capita payments to tribal members. Also the money is used to build up their tribal infrastructure: roads, water, sewer system, and a state-of-the-art fire station that can help nearby communities, should the need arise.

Norman's and Amos's sons, Stanley and Glynn, tribal chairman and vice-chairman, carry on the generous legacy of their fathers. Through their generosity the tribe has donated and loaned millions of dollars to other less fortunate tribes. Their contributions to educational programs remain unprecedented and unmatched. The Crooks family has always maintained their cultural identity. Every year they contribute financial assistance to over sixty tribes and educational facilities for *wacipis* or powwows. They say, "It is our cultural and social tradition to assist those in need. We take pride in our community's ongoing efforts to help others."

Other former students of Pipestone went on to become nationally recognized. Dennis Banks and Eddie Benton-Banai were among the founding members of AIM (American Indian Movement). Eddie Benton-Banai wrote *The Mishomis Book: The Voice of the Ojibway* in 1988. It is a beautiful book about Ojibwe culture, legends, and spirituality. Even the call of Hollywood was not lost on our boys. Mark Banks and Billy Daydodge became actors who played the role of Indians in numerous westerns. And Homer William, of the Sisseton Wahpeton reservation, retired at a high rank in the BIA. For me, as for many others, the education and care we received at Pipestone were an integral part of our success in life.

Appendix 1

Excerpt from Gaylord V. Reynolds, "The History of Pipestone Indian School" (master's thesis, University of South Dakota, 1952), 32–36.

Student B: Male, one-half-blood Indian. Entered school in 1931. Family status— Mother ill with cancer; father frequently deserts family; family held together by grandfather who recently died. Boy on probation from his home county. Entered Pipestone Indian School in the third grade. Completed the eighth grade a *C* student.

Student C: Male, three-fourths-blood Indian. Entered school 1939. Parents separated; father remarried; stepmother did not get along with him. Sent to Pipestone. Made better than average grades while there. Ran away from school. Did not complete his elementary education. No further report.

Student D: Male, three-fourths-blood Indian. Entered school in 1940, grade four. Mother dead and father trying to raise the family. Impossible home situation. Father died while the boy was in school. Boy completed eighth grade at Pipestone. One of the few follow-up cases where information is available. The boy is now a junior in an Indian vocational high school and well on his way to becoming a good citizen.

Student E: Male, one-fourth-blood Indian. Entered Pipestone in 1942. Very unstable home. Father threatened to commit suicide and take the whole family with him. Boy accepted at Pipestone. Sister in an asylum for feebleminded.

Mother (a white woman) died. Student completed his work at Pipestone with C-plus grades. No further information.

Student F: Male, one-half-degree Indian. Entered school in 1943. Children deserted by parents. Given home by grandfather until he could unite them with parents. Father murdered a man he found with his wife. Children sent to Pipestone. Student ran away from school before completing seventh grade. No further report.

Student J: Male, one-fourth-blood Indian. Entered Pipestone in the third grade. Father unknown. A boy with a very good mind. Made good grades. Ran away on one or two occasions but came back to complete his work. Now successfully completing his second year at an Indian school of higher education.

Student L: Female, one-half-blood Indian. Entered Pipestone in the second grade, and was here until completion of her elementary work. Parents were drunkards and home life was unbearable. Infrequent visits by parents (whom both children disliked) upset her. Several escapades which made teachers despair of her future. Settled down, completed her work, and is making good grades in secondary school.

Student N: Female, fullblood Indian. Entered Pipestone in 1941. Parents both habitual drunkards to whom the children mean nothing. Spent a full eight years at Pipestone, won a DAR [Daughters of the American Revolution] award, and is now well on her way to becoming a successful leader in the field of Indian education.

Student O: Female, one-half-blood Indian. Entered the fourth grade at Pipestone in 1945. Father unknown. Mother an inmate of the school for feebleminded. Progress of the girl, while slow, was satisfactory. She completed the eighth grade, but no further report on her is forthcoming.

Student Q: Female, one-half-degree Indian. Entered the seventh grade at Pipestone. Twelve children in the family. Mother dead. Father drunk every weekend. This student completed the eighth grade at Pipestone with above average grades. Has gone on to secondary school and has successfully completed her junior year.

Student S: Female, fullblood Indian. Entered sixth grade at Pipestone. Mother had no schooling and did not speak English. Father neglected children. Much drinking in the home, a one-room home with eight people living in it. In spite of these handicaps, this girl successfully completed her eighth grade work. Further progress has not been checked or recorded.

Student T: Female, one-half-degree Indian. Entered the fifth grade at Pipestone after having been out a full year. The children of this family were abandoned by their parents and lived with the grandparents. Parents showed no interest in girl whatever. This girl possessed a brilliant mind and was a straight *A* student. An educational test, given at the end of her seventh year, showed her capable of doing second-year work in high school. Did not return for her eighth grade work. Much to the author's disappointment, it has been impossible to trace further advancement of this student.

The above cases give a cross section of the types of student personnel who attend Pipestone Indian School. It should be noted that students are helped to overcome sordid background experiences to complete their elementary education. The average IQ of Pipestone students would run about five points lower than the average of the students in a public school.[1] This could probably be attributed to lack of proper background. Yet, it is found that once these students become used to school as a steady routine and have the proper leadership they become just as capable and efficient as the public school students.[2] Valuable time is lost each fall when the student, who has been home for the summer months or who is entering a boarding school for the first time, must acclimate himself to the daily routine of school.[3] Once adjusted, the progress of most of the students is rapid.[4] One drawback to the education of the Indian child is parental indifference to his or her education. Where the Indian child attends a public school, this results in a high percentage of absenteeism.[5] When an Indian child enters a boarding school such as Pipestone, the first few weeks must be spent in awakening the child and arousing within him the desire for higher learning. Once this is accomplished, the student progresses normally and at about the same rate of learning as the public school student.[6]

Appendix 2

A Brief History of "The Pipestone Indian School," Courtesy Pipestone County Museum.

The Indian School was apparently the idea of an early pioneer. So far as records show, the first suggestion that the government establish an Indian School on the Pipestone Reservation was made in 1875 by D. C. Whitehead, who was interested in developing the settlement here. While many expressed approval of the idea, it was fifteen years before an active campaign was launched to establish such a school.

This idea of an Indian Training School was in accordance with a federal policy toward the American Indian in the 1890s. The Indians were urged to be assimilated into the white society by breaking up tribal ways of life and educating them through traditional white means—a school system. In 1891 a bill passed Congress which appropriated $30,000 for the Pipestone school. Provision was made for one building. The contract for erection of the structure was awarded to J. M. Poorbaugh, who had it completed by the fall of 1892. It was built of locally quarried Sioux quartzite.

In February 1893, the Pipestone Indian Training School opened for admission of pupils. The first children enrolled were a small party transferred from the Menominee boarding school in Wisconsin, which had been abolished. At that time the school plant consisted of a single large building, heated with stoves and poorly lighted with kerosene lamps. In this one building were the pupils' and employees' quarters, kitchen and dining rooms; everything that went into the making of the somewhat complex life and work of an Indian boarding school. The school grew to consist of fifty-five buildings, including the farm and cottages, eleven of which were of the locally quarried Sioux quartzite.

C. J. Crandell, the school's first superintendent, opened the school Feb. 2, 1893. The class admitted at that time consisted of six who were transferred from the Keshena, Wisconsin, boarding school. The students ranged in ages from six to eighteen. They came from various tribes: Sioux, Chippewa, Sac and Fox, Oneida, Pottawatomie, Omaha, Winnebago, Gros Ventre, Arickaree, and Mandan. They were furnished with food, clothing, transportation, medical and dental services, and vocational and academic education. In turn, the students were responsible for all domestic chores, such as washing, cooking, sewing, and gardening. They also maintained the school grounds and dairy farm.

The federal policy toward the Indian changed in the 1950s. The government offered the states an arrangement under which the states would try to integrate the Indians into white schools and among the white workers. Relief services would be handled by the state welfare department, and the government would give the state an amount of money determined on a per capita basis. As the policy developed and the department worked out the closing of the Pipestone school, Minnesota children were sent to Wakpalla and elsewhere, and grades 9, 8, 7, and 6 were closed. Finally the training school was closed entirely, and only the necessary caretakers remained.

Many more or less feasible suggestions for use of the property were put forward, all in turn rejected. It was known that the Indian Department was willing to dispose of the property at a price set by the department or by special services. Pipestone city councilmen were anxious to add the fine well to the city water systems. The Sportsmen's Club wanted land in the northwest corner of the reservation, not a part of the campus. Negotiations dragged on for about four years before, at long last, an agreement was reached. The city of Pipestone completed arrangements to purchase the campus buildings, the well and water tower and all of the land (outside the national monument area) except 117 acres. This was finally reserved and given to the game and fish department.

The conservation area included two small lakes, and plans called for the improvement of both of these and for improvement in general on the entire tract. The city of Pipestone bought the 56-building Indian school campus and equipment for $45,000. Before the deed was actually executed, the Department of

Indian Affairs granted the city right of entry to the 36-acre tract, which had been vacant since May 1955.

Plans were quickly made to sell nine of the frame barns, garages, and other small buildings to clear the grounds and make them more attractive. An auction sale was held Jan. 25, 1958. The total price obtained came to $3,585. All buildings had to be removed from the premises by April 1. The Good Samaritan Society bid for the hospital and related buildings. The society now has a large home for the elderly at the site. The city later sold much of the remaining site to the vocational school, for $1.

Afterword

Laurence M. Hauptman

I have known Adam Fortunate Eagle for nearly forty years, and every time I listen to him, he surprises me, often throwing me a curveball. While some view him as a wily coyote, an Indian trickster, I view him quite differently.[1] To me, Fortunate Eagle, an enrolled Red Lake Ojibwe and adopted Crow, is the epitome of the contrary warrior, always challenging what has been blindly accepted. His contributions to the contemporary Indian world have been widely recognized, including in the writings of such American Indian intellectuals as the late Vine Deloria, Jr.[2] Unfortunately, because he frequently goes against the grain, Fortunate Eagle has often been dismissed or unfairly subjected to intense criticism, condemnation, and political retaliation in both the Indian and non-Indian worlds.[3]

In this memoir, Fortunate Eagle focuses on his ten years, from 1935 to 1945, as a student at the Pipestone Indian Training School, a major off-reservation federal Indian boarding school in southwestern Minnesota. Never an apologist for Washington-directed Indian policies, Fortunate Eagle nevertheless challenges some of our long-held assumptions about federal Indian educational policies and young children's experiences at these boarding schools. Young Adam as well as six of his siblings—Alton, Curtis, Myra, Stanley, Viola, and Wallace—all attended Pipestone. Adam arrived at the school as a five-year-old in the midst of the Great Depression. Seventy-five years later, Fortunate Eagle offers this poignant tale of his Pipestone years—the most richly detailed first-person account of life at a federally administered boarding school during the Indian New Deal period ever to be published.

I first met Adam Fortunate Eagle, then known as Adam Nordwall, in 1973. In May of that year, Fortunate Eagle, best known then for his leadership of the Alcatraz Island takeover three and one-half years earlier, came to speak at SUNY New Paltz at a major conference. In Native American regalia, he dramatically addressed a banquet audience of 350 people, including curious students, faculty, and community members who had never seen a "real Indian" before, as well as reservation and off-reservation Indians from all over the Northeast. With an engaging style, the Ojibwe taught lessons to his audience that have reverberated throughout the Northeast for years, namely that Native peoples are still here and that they are intelligent human beings whose rights and concerns must be respected. One might recall that in early 1973 the media depicted American Indian Movement (AIM) activists, who had used armed force to take over Wounded Knee, as the only voice of protest in the American Indian world; Fortunate Eagle, however, in his typical contrary warrior style, took a far different approach, addressing his audience not with accusatory anti-white "Buffalo speeches," typical for the times, but by employing Indian humor to make his points.

At a time when New York State colleges offered virtually no courses in Native American history, Fortunate Eagle's presentation had a dramatic influence on what was to develop. Today many colleges in New York offer a course on American Indians. Indeed, my own long-time presence at SUNY New Paltz can be directly connected to Fortunate Eagle's stunning appearance and his message at that 1973 conference. While Fortunate Eagle's résumé includes his roles as leading activist in the age of Red Power politics, distinguished artist, raconteur of note, and writer of well-received articles and books, I consider him first and foremost a brilliant educator. Hence, it was not surprising to me that in May 2001, Fortunate Eagle received an honorary degree from the State University of New York at New Paltz for his lifetime achievements as an educator.[4]

Long before his appearance on the SUNY New Paltz campus that May evening in 1973, Fortunate Eagle had been educating Californians, both Indians and non-Indians, about American Indians and their concerns. He had come to the state with his wife, Bobbie, in 1951, a few years before the federal Indian relocation program started bringing thousands of reservation

Indians into American cities. This assimilationist tactic was part of the overall policy of federal withdrawal, or termination, ostensibly intended to integrate American Indians into the American body politic and out of poverty-stricken rural communities. Throughout the 1950s and early 1960s, Fortunate Eagle established himself as a successful businessman, but he never forgot his Ojibwe roots at Red Lake, Minnesota, nor the lessons of survival he had learned during his fifteen years at two federal boarding schools—Pipestone Indian Training School and Haskell Institute. In California, he helped found the United Bay Area Council in 1962 and the Intertribal Council of California in 1965.[5] By this time, he had become a leading advocate of urban Indians as well as a mentor to young Indian newcomers to the San Francisco–Oakland Bay community.

When Texas millionaire Lamar Hunt announced plans in 1969 to convert Alcatraz Island into an amusement park and after the American Indian Center in San Francisco burned to the ground, Fortunate Eagle conceived of a plan to seize and occupy the island to bring attention to the plight of Indians nationwide. This occurred while he was teaching a class on American Indians at California State University, Hayward, a position he held until 1973.[6] Many students from both Hayward and San Francisco State College ended up taking part in the occupation of the island, which began in November 1969. Fortunate Eagle led the drafting of the Alcatraz "Proclamation of Indians of All Tribes"—and became directly involved in negotiating with federal representatives sent by the Nixon White House to attempt to end the seizure. President Nixon's famous policy directive of July 8, 1970, formally ended the federal Termination Policy.[7]

By the time Fortunate Eagle came to New Paltz in 1973, instead of exhibiting the angry militancy that was in style at the time, he used his keen sense of humor to bring his points across—humor that characterizes his speech and writings to this day. After all, this was the same man who conceived the idea that Indians were so desperate on reservations and in urban areas that they would be better off breaking into an abandoned maximum security prison, which was in total disrepair, in the middle of wind-swept San Francisco Bay! Without the stridency of other activists, Fortunate Eagle, a leading American

Indian intellectual, found practical ways to change things. He studied his audiences well beforehand and tried to disengage them with his humor. Although this style of protest has led some to dismiss him as simply an Indian trickster, he was and is totally in earnest about wanting to improve life in Native America. Much like I. F. Stone with a sense of humor, Fortunate Eagle constantly exposes the hypocrisy of United States Indian policies. By 1973 Fortunate Eagle clearly understood that the "media was the message" that could enlighten the public to the real grievances of American Indians. Consequently, he cultivated relationships with key reporters such as Tim Findley of the *San Francisco Chronicle*.[8] On September 24, 1973, after alerting the newspapers in Rome that he was arriving at Leonardo da Vinci Airport, he boldly came off the tarmac and proclaimed Italy for American Indians by "right of discovery." Then he created a Bureau of Italian Affairs. The incident was immediately reported throughout the world. Once again, Fortunate Eagle, the educator, had caught the attention of the public, challenging popular misconceptions with his keen sense of humor, this time teaching a lesson about the so-called Age of Discovery.[9]

Thus, *Pipestone*, with its radically different perspective on Indian boarding schools, is not surprising to me. Once again, Fortunate Eagle is challenging the usual interpretation. Although he is much more serious here than I have found him to be in the past, he still uses his unique sense of humor to educate.

‡ ‡ ‡

The federal Indian boarding school era began in 1879. In that year, a former Union Army captain and frontier officer, Richard Henry Pratt, was given permission to educate Indian children at an abandoned military outpost in Carlisle, Pennsylvania. He had earlier enrolled former Plains Indian prisoners-of-war at Hampton Institute, Virginia, a boarding school founded by Samuel Chapman Armstrong for the education of former slaves. Pratt considered Indians to be intelligent human beings who needed to be quickly detribalized, acculturated as rapidly as possible by the curriculum and the military-style discipline of boarding schools, immersed into white society by outing programs, and transformed into valuable tax-paying citizens whose rights would be protected under American law. In Pratt's mind, the old Indian ways were totally outmoded and unsuitable for the age. He convinced Secretary of the Interior Carl Schurz that his ideas fit into established federal policies of bringing "civilization" to Indians through a multifaceted plan that had its roots in the early days of the republic. This campaign to assimilate the Indians was based on the generally accepted assumption that it was possible to "kill the Indian but save the man." In this spirit, Pratt founded the famous United States Indian Industrial School at Carlisle, Pennsylvania. Carlisle became the model for other federal boarding schools established in the next quarter century, including Pipestone Indian School, which opened in 1893.[10]

In the White Man's Image, a PBS documentary first broadcast in 1992, gave the impression that each of these institutions did not change much over the decades, reflecting Pratt's original intent, despite being founded and operated at different times; having different administrators and teachers with varying temperaments and educational philosophies; enrolling students of different ages and genders; and being located in different places with differing Indian populations. The documentary portrayed boarding school experience from one decade to another in a sterile, unchanging way, placing its emphasis on bells, military-style discipline, and detribalization. It made no mention of the school's Indian employees. Teachers were pictured merely as agents of assimilation who had no real concern for the children; disciplinarians as sadistic ogres; and school superintendents as distant and unfeeling, indifferent to the welfare of their charges. The documentary stressed the psychological trauma caused by removing children from their native environments, an experience that scarred Indians and their communities for generations. Work details at the school, which occupied a significant part of the students' day, were described as joyless and exploitative. The documentary did not picture students as being allowed to return home for visits or for summer break; instead they appeared to be confined in a prison-like setting for years at a time or sent on "outings" to be exposed to whites in an effort to "civilize" them.[11]

At the same time, most recent studies over the past quarter century frequently give kudos to the children for their tactics of resistance, including running away or even attempts to sabotage the schools' programs. These works stress the students' brilliant ability to navigate and survive this harsh and demeaning world. David Wallace Adams's *Education for Extinction: American Indians and The Boarding School Experience, 1875–1928*, and most of the other recent literature, emphasizes unintended results of the federal assimilationist policy: by bringing Indian children together from different communities, a Pan-Indian consciousness developed and intertribal bonds were formed that later led to the creation of regional and national Indian organizations centering on political resistance.[12]

Although some case studies, as we shall see, have noted that individual Indian children had different experiences, including some positive ones, a generalized view continues to be presented or taught in today's classrooms, namely of dark, depressing institutions that intentionally afflicted pain on the Indian youngsters and permanently traumatized them for decades after graduation. In 2000, the Heard Museum hosted a major exhibit on these schools: "Away From Home: American Indian Boarding School Experiences." In one section of the exhibit catalogue, the editors insisted:

> Indian boarding schools were key components in the process of cultural genocide against Native cultures, and were designed to physically, ideologically, and emotionally remove Indian children from their families, homes, and tribal affiliations. From the moment students arrived at school, they could not "be Indian" in any way—culturally, artistically, spiritually, or linguistically. Repressive policies continued to varying degrees until the 1960s, when activism, reassertions of tribal sovereignty, and federal policies supporting tribal self-determination began to impact educational institutions and programs.[13]

There is some truth in the above statement, and Fortunate Eagle himself recognizes negative aspects about Pipestone. For example, he questions some of what was taught there. He wonders why Daniel Boone and Kit Carson were treated as heroes and how Manifest Destiny could have been good for the Indians. Yet at Pipestone he also first learns of the underside side of Manifest Destiny: he is exposed to the horrors that befell Indians in the Sioux War of 1876–77 and the Wounded Knee Massacre of 1890. And while food, clothing, and housing conditions were far superior to those on the reservation, the heat was turned off after 9 P.M. to save money, causing the temperature to drop to freezing inside the dormitory.

Despite his attention to problems at Pipestone, Fortunate Eagle does not offer the usual negative picture of federal boarding schools. He describes his friendship with Joe Crown, a Leech Lake Chippewa, and other lifelong friends he met at the school. He nostalgically looks back at his work in the bakery, the school dances and holiday pageants, as well as his interactions with members of different Native communities—from brawls with other Indian children to more formal boxing matches to listening to traditional storytelling by older Ho-Chunk, Lakota, Omaha, Oneida, and Sioux boys.

Overall, Fortunate Eagle's memoir enriches previous interpretations. First, he shows that Indian boarding school policies and policymakers did change and were not simply a reflection of Pratt's educational philosophy. Pratt was long gone, having been forced to step down as superintendent of Carlisle in 1904, fourteen years before Carlisle's formal closing. As Fortunate Eagle demonstrates, Pipestone School superintendent J. W. Balmer was no Pratt. During young Adam's tenure at the school, the children were allowed to speak their native languages; they were punished for cursing, not for speaking Ojibwe or Lakota. According to Fortunate Eagle, Balmer was honest with the students about the assimilationist aims of the school, although one wonders how younger students understood the word "assimilation" or the educational philosophy behind it. The reader gets the impression that Balmer was a Progressive educator, much like the innovative W. Carson Ryan and Willard W. Beatty, who headed the educational policies of the BIA after the Meriam Report of 1928 had exposed the horrendous conditions at certain federal Indian boarding schools.[14]

As Fortunate Eagle shows, students at Pipestone were not isolated. They had access to the town of Pipestone, where they could see movies and newsreels about the Nazis and the progress of the war effort. They could visit Roe's Trading Post, where they could learn about their history. They could also go off hunting pheasant and duck, go to the quarry a half mile from the school, and return home for the summer if there was some family supervision. During these summer sojourns, they could attend the July Fourth powwow and learn the traditions of their people. Because so many men were in the military at that time, the older Pipestone students, including Adam, actually served as firefighters during World War II. Indeed, Fortunate Eagle's boyhood visits to the famous Pipestone quarry and his working with the stone there, which has deep spiritual meaning to his people, inspired him to become a well-recognized pipestone calumet artist as well as an active leader in preserving the quarry, a special place in Ojibwe culture and religion.

Tribal affiliation also mattered. American Indians are diverse peoples and have had distinct histories. Hence, an Oneida at Carlisle or even Pipestone might have had quite a different school experience from that of a Lakota. For example, the Iroquois in New York and Wisconsin had had longer contact with non-Indians and educational institutions than most other Native Americans, and thus were more able to "play" the system. Unlike the Lakotas or Comanches, they had been at peace with whites since the American Revolution.

All of the previous boarding school accounts or studies, with one notable exception described below, minimize the existence and roles of Indian employees at these schools. Numerous American Indians were employees in the federal boarding school system. Many of them had attended Carlisle, Haskell, or other boarding schools. Fortunate Eagle clearly shows the lessons learned from these federal employees, especially Bea Burns, a Peoria Indian and the daughter of a chief. Burns served as a first-rate teacher who also supervised the boys in "Stink" dormitory. According to the memoir, she showed compassion and kindness to the youngsters at every turn and became their surrogate mother. Besides offering formal classroom instruction, she even taught the boys how to sew.

Fortunate Eagle also reveals the desperate economic, educational, and social conditions of Indian reservation life at the time, which early boarding school studies do not always stress sufficiently. Fortunate Eagle clearly paints his own family situation and the ways in which extreme poverty affected the Nordwall children. Pipestone personnel had to provide extra milk to new students arriving from reservations since they were suffering from malnutrition. When Adam's mother was forced to leave Red Lake because of her desperate economic situation and sought employment in Oregon, she enrolled him in Chemawa, another federal Indian boarding school; however, before going to this new school, young Adam hopped a bus and made his way back to Pipestone, to be welcomed by Mrs. Burns. Here, once again, Fortunate Eagle demonstrates his contrary nature, countering the usual image of Indian children resisting assimilation by running away from boarding schools. He actually ran back!

The boarding school system, as the author points out, worked on several levels. Pipestone and some of the other institutions were feeder schools that prepared younger students to go on to larger, more comprehensive boarding schools. Early in its lifespan, Pipestone became a feeder school for Carlisle, and later for neighboring Riggs (Flandreau), just across the South Dakota line, as well as Haskell Institute in Lawrence, Kansas, the latter a school that Adam attended after his early boyhood days. The two better-known off-reservation boarding schools—Carlisle and Haskell—often recruited promising musicians and athletes, especially star football players, from these feeder schools.

Much of the new scholarship on federal Indian boarding schools stems from 1983, with the publication of *Ethnic Identity and the Boarding School Experience of West-Central Oklahoma American Indians,* by Sally McBeth, an anthropologist who drew on fieldwork and interviews of graduates to explore the topic.[15] In 1984, Frederick E. Hoxie, largely employing a wide range of archival records, placed the boarding school experience into the overall framework of late nineteenth- and twentieth-century federal Indian policies. Unfortunately, while Hoxie's *A Final Promise: The Campaign to Assimilate the Indians, 1880–1920* provides a valuable overview of policy formation in the age of allotment, a reader cannot discern any Native voice in the work.[16] In 1988, Robert A. Trennert, Jr., published a major history of the Phoenix Indian School. Founded in 1891, the school was modeled on Carlisle. In his well-organized and thorough examination of archival records in Washington and at the Federal Records Center at Laguna, California, Trennert analyzes the years before 1935, the very year Fortunate Eagle entered Pipestone. Although bringing out important information about Phoenix and its policies, Trennert's work is largely an administrative history, focusing on its failings. Yet he does acknowledge, in keeping with what is demonstrated in Fortunate Eagle's memoir, that the Indian New Deal under Commissioner

Collier substantially changed the authoritarian nature of Phoenix and other federal boarding schools.[17]

In 1993, K. Tsianina Lomawaima analyzed the history of Chilocco Indian Agricultural School, founded in 1884 and located near Tulsa, Oklahoma. By employing interviews of Indians, mostly from rural Oklahoma, who attended the school from 1920 to 1940, her award-winning study presents a far different interpretation than that suggested by Fortunate Eagle's memoir. Lomawaima's father had been a student at Chilocco in the 1920s. She focuses almost exclusively on the dark side of federal Indian boarding schools, except for descriptions of student resistance to the indoctrination process. She shows how these students rebelled and/or navigated their way through a system that included harsh punishment, the exploitation of child labor, inadequate educational and vocational training, and gender stereotyping. She admits that some Chilocco students in this period count their schooldays as "the happiest and most care-free of their lives," but she concludes that their experiences were based only on "a few social and cultural variables" such as the pupil's age upon entering the school and "the stability of their home lives."[18] Casting a wide net that is quite distinct from Fortunate Eagle's Pipestone memoir, Lomawaima generalizes:

> Bureau of Indian Affairs boarding schools, especially in the years before World War I, were often harsh and repressive institutions. Students were not allowed to speak their own language or practice their own religion. Their contact with home and family was severely restricted. In many ways, they were made to feel inferior. [19]

The Rainy Mountain Boarding School in western Oklahoma opened in the same year as Pipestone. In his 1996 case study, Clyde Ellis provides a straightforward history of this school. Although his work is based largely on federal records and the Doris Duke Oral History Collection, the author also interviewed the last surviving graduate of the school as well as relatives of those who had attended. Ellis attempts to tie federal Indian educational policies to the pseudo-scientific racial theories that arose around World War I. He never satisfactorily explains why the school closed in 1920, and he makes questionable claims about changes in federal policies during the Progressive Era that do not hold up under careful scrutiny. Ellis reminds readers that not all boarding schools were distant from Indian communities. Some, such as Rainy Mountain, which was established within the Kiowa-Comanche Agency, were located within Indian communities. Ellis confirms recent research on the federal Indian boarding school at Oneida, Wisconsin, which opened in 1893 and closed in 1918, noting that the Indians of that agency protested the school's closing, suggesting greater Indian support for these community schools.[20]

In 1998, Brenda Child, an enrolled Ojibwe from Red Lake, the very reservation that is Fortunate Eagle's homeland, published her innovative work *Boarding School Seasons, 1900–1940*. This book stands apart from previous studies, since it does not over-rely on the writings of BIA personnel or interviews of only a handful of surviving alumni. Child examines the correspondence between parents, their children, and school administrators at Haskell, Flandreau, and Pipestone during a forty-year period. Using this approach, and having had relatives who attended each of these institutions as well as Carlisle, she is able to describe boarding school experiences in a unique way. Child brings up some of the usual negative assessments made about these schools: the poor treatment of students by teachers and administrators; the trauma of separating children from their home environment and culture; the inadequate medical care provided; the outmoded skills taught; and the complaints about the regimentation, food, and the excessive or exploitative work done by the students in support of the school operations, which occasionally led students to run away. However, unlike Fortunate Eagle, Child ignores the roles of Indian employees in the schools, suggesting, as had William Ahern before her, that jobs disappeared in the Indian Service after 1900 because of racial restrictions in hiring.[21]

In other ways, Child confirms what Fortunate Eagle suggests in his memoir. She points out that the decision to send children to these schools was based on pragmatism, not coercion, as it had been before 1920. She effectively shows that the Ojibwe's traditional abilities to take care of orphans and others less fortunate were severely undermined by their impoverished reservation existence. Their beleaguered situation led these American Indians to make practical decisions, namely to send their children away to survive. She rightly mentions the significant Meriam Report of 1928 and its criticism of these schools, as well as the Indian New Deal, which she views as a turning point in the history of these institutions. Unfortunately, she does not analyze these changes in any depth in her all-too-brief account. Child notes that during the Great Depression, student admissions to these schools swelled, causing overcrowding. Federal officials suggested giving priority to the poorest of the Indian poor, because of the growing number of impoverished families who desired to send their children to boarding schools and into better economic circumstances. This clearly fits with conditions that Fortunate Eagle portrays in his memoir.[22]

In conclusion, Child writes:

> The legacy of government boarding schools is still being sorted out in American Indian communities. The history is rife with complex emotions, and memories have remained strong for former students. Ojibwe families that disintegrated during the boarding school years were a vulnerable population, frayed by the arrival of diseases, death, extreme poverty, and the social ills that invaded reservation communities in the early twentieth century.[23s]

Child rightly points out, in agreement with Fortunate Eagle's view: "The schools designed to separate Indian families, dilute the influences of home and impose a new set of cultural values ironically helped many Ojibwe families to survive hard times and economic depression."[24]

Child's observation applies to Fortunate Eagle's family in particular. Except for Viola, his family members did survive and went on to do amazing things with their lives: Alton served in the U.S. Navy in World War II and Korea, and, after retirement, worked as BIA Area director in Muskogee, Oklahoma. Curtis served with distinction in World War II and Korea. He earned the Silver Star for heroism in the South Pacific in World War II, taking part in the major battles at Guadalcanal and Leyte Gulf as well as in the successful operations to shoot down Admiral Yamamoto's plane in 1944. After retiring from the Navy as Lieutenant Commander, Curtis worked for the BIA as superintendent at the Havasupai and Walapai reservations in Arizona. Stanley was a paratrooper in the famous 82nd Airborne in the Normandy invasion, earning the Purple

Heart and Bronze Star. During World War II, Wallace was in the U.S. Army, serving on the frontlines as a medic in both the North African campaign against Field Marshall Erwin Rommel and at Anzio Beach in the invasion of Italy. Unlike his brothers,' Adam's struggles were not on distant shores. In the early 1970s, he ran unsuccessfully for Congress. Later, he worked on behalf of the water rights of Nevada Indians who were challenging the Newlands Irrigation Project. In 1991, the Paiutes eventually received $41 million in a settlement act passed by Congress.[25]

In addition to Child's work, other recent studies have added to our knowledge of Indian boarding schools. Published in 1999, Scott Riney's study of the Rapid City Indian School also uses federal records and letters from pupils and parents. Riney draws conclusions similar to Child's, but also offers new information. Established in South Dakota in 1898 to assimilate the Lakotas, the Rapid City school was one of the smallest federal boarding schools until its closing in 1933. Although much of Riney's book is familiar, he nevertheless makes a major contribution by including an important chapter on Indian, mostly Lakota, and non-Indian employees at the school. In 1912, out of thirty-one employees at the school, only nine were Indians.[26] Some were renowned individuals, such as Chauncey Yellow Robe, the well-known Carlisle Indian school musician and movie actor, who served as a teacher and disciplinarian at Rapid City for a quarter century. Riney rightly suggests that these American Indian employees were in no position to "alter the purposes of the institution."[27] Impressively, he analyzes the qualifying tests, the salaries, the hiring processes, and the workload and responsibilities of each position, including teachers, clerks, matrons, disciplinarians, and menial assistants.[28]

In the past decade, other studies have added to our knowledge of these schools. Sally McBeth coedited the memoir of Esther Burnett Horne, who is of Wind River Shoshone ancestry and is the great-great-granddaughter of Sacajawea. Horne graduated from Haskell Institute in 1929. Her book, *Essie's Story: The Life and Legacy of a Shoshone Teacher*, contains passages that remind me of Fortunate Eagle's *Pipestone*. After graduating from Haskell, Horne became a long-time teacher in other Indian boarding schools. While her first-person account does not completely focus on boarding schools—its contents

range far and wide, including discussions of Sacajawea and other family history—Horne's description of life at Haskell in some ways parallels Fortunate
Eagle's memoir. She points out the benevolent aspects of the school, praising
two of her kindest teachers there, who were her role models when she started
teaching at other boarding schools. Horne also describes how children from
different reservations learned each other's traditions, fostering Pan-Indianism
and permanent friendships and alliances, which in many ways subverted the
overall aims of federal boarding schools.[29]

A far different perspective is presented in Cary C. Collins's 2007 edit-
ed volume, *Assimilation's Agent: My Life as a Superintendent in the Indian
Boarding School System,* which clearly shows the difficulty of operating these
schools prior to the Meriam Report's expose. This account, much of which
focuses on Superintendent Edwin L. Chalcraft's home area of the Northwest,
is a memoir of his service from 1883 to 1925. Chalcraft served as a school
superintendent at the Chemawa Indian Boarding School and at other
Oregon schools, including those on the Chehalis Indian Reservation and at
Siletz Indian Agency. He was also an administrator at the Puyallup Indian
School in Washington, at the Wind River School in Wyoming, and finally
at the Jones Male Academy at Hartshorne, Oklahoma, and was the Federal
Supervisor of Indian Schools in the Office of Indian Affairs from 1900 to
1904. Despite the book's compelling descriptions of Indian country in the
Northwest, the peripatetic superintendent's account must be read with
caution, since even Collins admits in his introduction that he believes the
account has been sanitized.[30]

While popular writers continue to write almost yearly, in an uncritical way,
about the great Indian football teams at Carlisle, historians more recently
have explored the subject of Indian boarding school athletics in greater depth.
Athletics, especially football, had different and often contradictory meanings to
school administrators and to Glenn Pop Warner, the football coach at Carlisle,
than to the American public, Native communities throughout the United States,
and the Indian football players themselves. On the one hand, the roots of contemporary Indian sports stereotypes can be traced back to the way Indian
boarding school athletes, especially at Carlisle, were depicted by the media.

On the other, these programs engendered pride among American Indians and are still favorably talked and written about in Indian communities. Indeed, the role of team sports—football, baseball, basketball, and track and field—at times actually reinforced traditional Indian group consciousness, instead of promoting the non-Indian's emphasis on individual achievement.[31] One study clearly shows that by the 1930s, the time period focused on in Pipestone, the BIA was consciously deemphasizing athletics at these schools.[32] Other aspects of Indian boarding schools have received scholarly attention, including musical programs, especially the nationally known marching bands at Carlisle and Haskell. These major musical programs have been the focus of two recent scholarly articles and a new book, John Troutman's *Indian Blues: American Indians and the Politics of Music, 1890–1934.*[33]

Although Fortunate Eagle relies on memories that are well over sixty years old, much of what he describes is confirmed in several interviews with Iroquois boarding school alumni whom I have had the privilege of meeting and/or interviewing in Wisconsin and New York over the past four decades. These students graduated from the schools in the 1930s and 1940s. Two specifically come to mind: Purcell Powless and Lloyd Elm. Purcell Powless, former Wisconsin Oneida tribal chairman, came to Pipestone in 1937 as a twelve-year-old, at the same time Adam was attending the school. In one interview, Powless was specific about how the school positively shaped his life. While his homesick brother ran away from the school, Powless remained there:

> Oneidas worked at Pipestone. My relatives Sherman Baird and Lilian [*sic*] Powless Baird worked there. Sherman worked as a custodian in the powerhouse and Lilian was the head of the laundry. Sherman was a really nice guy. When I was sent as punishment to the powerhouse, he let me smoke. Anderson Cornelius' sister Delia was a baker at the school and her daughter was a cook at the school. Pemberton Doxtator was a night watchman there. Life at the school was good compared to home. No chores. I didn't have to cut kindling wood or the stove. We had steam heat. We had nice warm beds. We didn't have to get up and haul water . . . We had pretty good food, three meals a day. It was like going into the military. I received new clothing—shoes, shirts, jackets, for winter. At home I had to work on my father's thirty-acre truck farm, my grandfather's homestead. I had to do my chores before I could

go swimming in Duck Creek [on the Oneida reservation]. At school I worked in the laundry or on the school farm where I cleaned the barn, fed the cattle, and picked the corn. We worked half a day and the other half we attended classes. I hear they forbade our language at these schools, but it didn't affect me since I didn't know my language. The Winnebago [Ho-Chunk] and Sioux spoke their language in small groups at the school and yet no one bothered them.[34]

Lloyd Elm, an Onondaga elder and Professor of Education at SUNY Buffalo State College, went to Haskell as a fourteen-year-old, just after Adam's graduation from that school. Elm, a nationally known Indian educator who has been honored by the National Education Association, stated unequivocally to me as well as in addresses at Native American conferences that being sent to Haskell Institute by his parents actually saved his life and shaped his ideas about the need for and desirability of all-Indian schools. He put his ideas into practice, directing the Native American School in Buffalo and the Mounds Park All Nations Magnet School in St. Paul, Minnesota.[35]

Pipestone Indian Training School, which closed in 1952, did have a very complex history since its opening in 1893. Yes, its mission was to help "end the Indian problem" by assimilating children and encouraging them to leave the reservation; however, what far-off Washington policymakers intended and wanted to be carried out was never fully implemented by certain school administrators and personnel "on the ground." Fortunate Eagle makes clear that by the mid-1930s to mid-1940s, Pratt's ideas were long gone, at least at Pipestone. Indeed, some of the school's graduates' accomplishments seem in complete opposition to the school's initial mission statement. For example, Purcell Powless, who served his Wisconsin Oneidas with distinction for twenty-three years as tribal chairman, helped his Indian nation revive its community's economy, landbase, and influence in the Midwest; while Fortunate Eagle, armed without bullets in his political actions and writings, savored his role as a contrary warrior. Instead of fighting with footnotes, the historians' general method of attack, Adam Fortunate Eagle has intelligently found a way to disengage and disarm his enemies, exposing their hypocrisies by his mere presence—with a smile, a humorous phrase or two that pokes holes into past assumptions, and all his memorable lines.

Notes

INTRODUCTION

1. Northwest Ordinance of 1789.
2. S. Lyman Tyler, *A History of Indian Policy* (Washington, D.C.: U.S. Department of Interior, Bureau of Indian Affairs, 1973), 56.
3. Ibid.
4. Kenneth Phelps, *John Collier's Crusade for Indian Reform* 1920–1954 (Tucson: University of Arizona Press, 1977), 128.
5. Letter from J. W. Balmer to Gaylord V. Reynolds, April 19, 1952. Quoted in Gaylord V. Reynolds, "The History of Pipestone Indian School" (master's thesis, University of South Dakota, August 1952).

LIFE AT PIPESTONE INDIAN BOARDING SCHOOL
All sources courtesy Pipestone County Historical Society unless otherwise noted.

1. *Pipestone Star,* November 1, 1940, 1.
2. Pipestone School Quarterly Report, September 30, 1936.
3. *Pipestone Star,* December 26, 1939, 8.
4. Pipestone School Quarterly Report, June 30, 1939.
5. *Pipestone Star,* December 20, 1940, 1.
6. "Boarding School Report of Menus," *Pipestone Star,* December 26, 1939, 8.
7. *Pipestone Star,* May 20, 1941, 1.
8. *Pipestone Star,* May 27, 1941, 1.
9. Author interviews with adult Joe Crown and other men to verify treatment at St. Mary's Catholic Mission School.
10. "Boarding School Report of Menus," *Pipestone Star,* December 26, 1939, 8.
11. *Pipestone Star,* April 23, 1940, 1.
12. *Pipestone Star,* August 3, 1943, 1.
13. *Pipestone Star,* February 16, 1937, 8.
14. *Pipestone Star,* September 24, 1943, 1.
15. *Pipestone Star,* July 30, 1943, 1.
16. *Pipestone Star,* February 29, 1944, 1.

LIFE AFTER PIPESTONE INDIAN BOARDING SCHOOL

1. U.S. Army Secret Document, "Record of Participation of 508th Parachute Infantry in Normandy Operations from 6 June to 15 July 1944."

APPENDIX 1

1. Tests given at Pipestone Indian School and compared with records of Pipestone Public Schools.

2. Results of tests given over a period of three years, 1949–52.

3. Comparison of achievement tests at beginning of the school with results of tests given the previous spring.

4. Advancement recorded in achievement tests given at beginning and end of school year.

5. Study of attendance records of students who have attended public school and then enter Pipestone Indian School.

6. Comparison of achievement records of students in Pipestone Indian School with achievement records of students in Pipestone public schools.

AFTERWORD

1. Sam McManus, "Profile: Adam Fortunate Eagle Nordwall: Bay Area's Trickster Grandfather of Radical Indian Movement," *San Francisco Chronicle,* October 21, 2002. Tim Findley, the former reporter for the *San Francisco Chronicle* who covered the Alcatraz takeover, befriended Fortunate Eagle and later collaborated with him in his accounts of the occupation. Findley clearly saw that some Indians misconstrued Fortunate Eagle's levity—"joke-medicine"—and did not recognize that he was trying to educate by using humor. Findley, "Alcatraz Recollections," in *American Indian Activism: Alcatraz to the Longest Walk,* ed. Troy Johnson, Joane Nagel, and Duane Champagne (Urbana: University of Illinois Press, 1997), 74–87.

2. Vine Deloria, Jr., foreword to *Heart of the Rock: The Indian Invasion of Alcatraz,* by Adam Fortunate Eagle with Tim Findley (Norman: University of Oklahoma Press, 2002), ix–xi. Right from the beginning of the seizure of Alcatraz, Deloria, who himself understood "joke-medicine," rightly viewed this occupation as a watershed in contemporary Indian history. See Deloria, "This Country Was a Lot Better Off When the Indians Were Running the Country," *New York Times Magazine,* March 8, 1970.

3. Fortunate Eagle suffered as a result of his outspoken nature and leadership role at Alcatraz. He was subjected to IRS scrutiny and was later federally prosecuted for allegedly selling eagle feathers. Although he was not convicted in a jury trial, he was forced to pay a substantial fine as a result of a later civil action. Jerry Reynolds, "A Myth in the Making: Alcatraz at 35," *Indian Country Today,* November 19, 2004. Fortunate Eagle has been severely criticized as a "publicity seeker" by some, including La Nada Means Boyer, as well as by other members of the American Indian Movement. It should be noted that AIM, newly formed in Minnesota prisons in 1968, was not involved in the planning or initial takeover of Alcatraz, although some of those who occupied Alcatraz,

such as Boyer and John Trudell, later became AIM activists. Fortunate Eagle's role at
Alcatraz and in the Bay Area Indian community has been minimized by some writers, such as Troy R. Johnson, who have relied on his critics for information or those,
such as Paul Chaat Smith and Robert Allen Warrior, who did not bother to interview
him. For Boyer's criticism, see McManus, "Profile: Adam Fortunate Eagle Nordwall."
For Johnson's writings, see *The Occupation of Alcatraz Island: Indian Self-Determination
and the Rise of Indian Activism* (Urbana: University of Illinois, 1996). For Smith's and
Warrior's writings, see their cowritten volume *Like a Hurricane: The Indian Movement
from Alcatraz to Wounded Knee* (New York: New Press, 1996). My harsh conclusions
are based on my own archival research in the Alcatraz materials at the Federal Records
Center at San Bruno, California, and in Record Group 220, Records of the National
Council on Indian Opportunity, National Archives, Washington, D.C. Before his death
in 1980, Commissioner of Indian Affairs Louis R. Bruce, Jr., had also become my friend
and a revealing source about the Nixon administration's Indian policy. My many discussions over the years with Gerald Hill, the former Wisconsin Oneida attorney and
former head of the American Indian Trial Lawyers Association, who taught at the
Alcatraz school during the occupation, also proved helpful to my understanding of
both Fortunate Eagle and the significance of the event. In 1999, Fortunate Eagle's role
was finally acknowledged when the Smithsonian put him on the cover of its magazine
and therein featured an article on the thirty-year anniversary of the Alcatraz occupation. Ben Winton, "Alcatraz: Indian Land," *Native Peoples* 13 (Fall 1999): 26–36.

4. Fortunate Eagle said to the graduates: "When you have a goal in mind or a mission in
life, you must pursue it in spite of the sometimes-overwhelming odds that stand in your
way. If you have morality and a sense of justice on your side, you can prevail." Quoted
in Anthony P. Musso and Lori O'Toole, "1185 Say Farewell to SUNY Community,"
Poughkeepsie Journal, May 21, 2001.

5. Fortunate Eagle with Findley, *Heart of the Rock*, 3–62; Findley, "Alcatraz Recollections";
Fortunate Eagle, interviews by Laurence M. Hauptman, December 23, 29, 2008.

6. Deloria, "Foreword."

7. For further insights into Nixon's Indian policies, see Leonard Garment, *Crazy Rhythm:
From Brooklyn and Jazz to Nixon's White House, Watergate, and Beyond* (New York:
DaCapo Press, 1996), 223–28. See also Hauptman, "Finally Acknowledging Native
Peoples: American Indian Policies since the Nixon Administration," in *"They Made Us
Many Promises": The American Indian Experience, 1524 to the Present*, ed. Philip Weeks
(Wheeling, Ill.: Harlan Davidson, 2002), 210–27.

8. Findley, "Alcatraz Recollections."

9. See, for example, Albin Krebs, "Notes on People," *New York Times*, September 25, 1973, 36.

10. For Pratt, see his own memoir: *Battlefield and Classroom: Four Decades with the
American Indian, 1867–1904*, ed. Robert M. Utley (New Haven: Yale University Press,
1964). The best study of Carlisle is an unpublished Ph.D. dissertation by Genevieve
Bell, "Telling Stories out of School: The Carlisle Industrial School, 1879–1918" (Palo

Alto, Calif.: Stanford University Press, 1998). For Hampton Institute, which was not a federal Indian boarding school but accepted numerous Indian children for nearly a half century, see Donal F. Lindsey, *Indians at Hampton Institute, 1877–1923* (Urbana: University of Illinois Press, 1995).

11. *In the White Man's Image,* written and directed by Christine Lesiak, documentary for PBS (WGBH), "The American Experience" series, 1992. Despite its limitations, Lesiak's documentary is highly recommended by the two major textbooks in American Indian history: R. David Edmunds, Frederick E. Hoxie, and Neal Salisbury, *The People: A History of Native America* (Boston: Houghton Mifflin, 2007), 493; and Colin Calloway, *First Peoples: A Documentary Survey of American Indian History,* 3rd ed. (New York: Bedford Books/St. Martin's, 2008), 618.

12. David Wallace Adams, *Education for Extinction: American Indians and the Boarding School Experience, 1875–1928* (Lawrence: University Press of Kansas, 1995).

13. Editors' introduction to *Away From Home: American Indian Boarding School Experiences,* ed. Margaret L. Archuleta, Brenda J. Child, and K. Tsianina Lomawaima (Phoenix: Heard Museum, 2000), 19.

14. Margaret Szasz, *Education and the American Indian: The Road to Self-Determination since 1928,* 3rd ed. (Albuquerque, University of New Mexico Press, 1999).

15. Sally McBeth, *Ethnic Identity and the Boarding School Experience of West-Central Oklahoma American Indians* (Washington, D.C.: University Press of America, 1983).

16. Frederick E. Hoxie, *A Final Promise: The Campaign to Assimilate the Indians, 1880–1920* (Lincoln: University of Nebraska Press, 1984).

17. Robert A. Trennert, Jr., *The Phoenix Indian School: Forced Assimilation in Arizona, 1891–1935* (Norman: University of Oklahoma Press, 1988); and his "Corporal Punishment and the Politics of Indian Reform," *History of Education Quarterly* 29 (Winter 1989): 595–617

18. K. Tsianina Lomawaima, *They Called It Prairie Light: The Story of Chilocco Indian School* (Lincoln: University of Nebraska Press, 1994), xiv.

19. *Ibid.*

20. Clyde Ellis, *To Change Them Forever: Indian Education at the Rainy Mountain Boarding School, 1893–1920* (Norman: University of Oklahoma Press, 1996). For Wisconsin efforts to save their federal Indian boarding school, see Patricia Stovey, "Opportunities at Home: Laura Cornelius Kellogg and Village Industrialization," in *The Oneida Indians in the Age of Allotment, 1860–1920,* ed. Laurence M. Hauptman and L. Gordon McLester III (Norman: University of Oklahoma Press, 2006), 150–54.

21. Brenda J. Child, *Boarding School Seasons: American Indian Families, 1900–1940* (Lincoln: University of Nebraska Press, 1998). For Wilbert Ahern's study, see "An Experiment Aborted: Returned Indian Students in the Indian Service, 1881–1908," *Ethnohistory* 44 (1997): 263–304.

22. Child, *Boarding School Seasons,* 21.

23. *Ibid,* 100.

24. *Ibid.*

25. Fortunate Eagle, interviews by Hauptman, December 16, 23, 2008, January 12, 2009. Gerald Kitzmann served as Fortunate Eagle's congressional campaign manager. Kitzmann, interviews by Hauptman, January 6, 2009.

26. Scott Riney, *The Rapid City Indian School,* 1898–1933 (Norman: University of Oklahoma Press, 1999).

27. *Ibid,* 168.

28. *Ibid,* 167–92.

29. Esther Burnett Horne and Sally McBeth, *Essie's Story: The Life and Legacy of a Shoshone Teacher* (Lincoln: University of Nebraska Press, 1998).

30. Edwin L. Chalcraft, *Assimilation's Agent: My Life as a Superintendent in the Indian Boarding School System,* ed. Cary C. Collins (Lincoln: University of Nebraska Press, 2004).

31. David Wallace Adams, "More than a Game: The Carlisle Indians Take to the Gridiron, 1893–1917," *Western Historical Quarterly* 32 (Spring 2001): 25–54.

32. John Bloom, *To Show What an Indian Can Do: Sports at Native American Boarding Schools* (Minneapolis: University of Minnesota Press, 2000).

33. Laurence M. Hauptman, "From Carlisle to Carnegie Hall: The Musical Career of Dennison Wheelock," in *The Oneida Indians in the Age of Allotment,* 112–38; and Hauptman, "Marszem Do Cywilizacji: Orkiestra Szkoly dia Indian w Carlisle za czasow." ["Marching Bands and Band Music at Carlisle during the Pratt Era"] *Tawacin* [University of Warsaw—Poland] No. 2 (82): 18–26. John W. Troutman, *Indian Blues: American Indians and the Politics of Music,* 1890–1934 (Norman: University of Oklahoma Press, 2009).

34. Purcell Powless, "My School Days," in *The Oneida Indians in the Age of Allotment,* 84–85.

35. Lloyd Elm, interview by Hauptman, July 31, 2005, St. Lawrence University, Canton, New York; NEA homepage, news release, June 16, 2002, www.nea.org/nr/nr020610. html. I first heard Dr. Elm speak about his favorable experiences at Haskell in December 1972, during a conference at Herkimer County Community College. When he received his service award from the National Education Association for his contributions to Native American education, he also stressed his positive experience at Haskell.

Glossary

Ah waah	You're pulling my leg, I don't believe you, you're kidding me
Amabese	Handsome
Ho wah	Wow! My goodness! Oh my!
Ish	Yuck
Migizi	Eagle
Mii gwitch	Thank you
Ow-wah-high	Ouch! That really hurts!
Wacipis	Powwows
Waynebosho	Legendary shape-shifter; good spirit
Weendigo	Cannibal monster that roars
Weesinin	Let's eat
Weh-eh	Namesake